## SCORING

**Basic:** When a team successfully completes a Basic charade (a TV, Movie, Song or Lightning Round charade that does not have a star next to it), that team scores 2 points and takes two yellow (one point) chips.

**\*:** When a team successfully completes a charade marked with a star, that team receives the number of points equal to their dice roll. For example: Team A rolls a 4, moves and successfully completes a charade marked with a star. That team scores 4 points and takes 4 points worth of chips for that charade.

**Play Off:** The team that wins the Play Off rolls the die and scores DOUBLE the amount shown on the die. For example: Team B wins the Play Off and rolls a 5. They would double the points and take 10 points worth of chips for that charade.

**Pressman®**
Games people play. Together.

We appreciate your comments and questions concerning The Charade Game. Please send all correspondence to:

Pressman Toy Corp.
Dept. Charade
745 Joyce Kilmer Ave.
New Brunswick, NJ 08901

a Playtoy Industries
le Games, Ltd.
Corporation, New York, N.Y.

3501/8533

*All inquiries should be addressed to:*
Barron's Educational Series, Inc.
250 Wireless Boulevard
Hauppauge, New York 11788
http://www.barronseduc.com

Library of Congress Catalog Card No. 99-28053

International Standard Book No. 0-7641-0818-2

**Library of Congress Cataloging-in-Publication Data**

Kenda, Margaret.
    Word wizardry / Margaret Kenda and William Kenda.
        p.      cm.
    Includes index.
    Summary: Discusses the nature of language and words
    and suggests activities that use words in various forms,
    including name games, fancy lettering, word puzzles,
    and secret messages.
    ISBN 0-7641-0818-2
    1. Children—Language Juvenile literature.   2. Education,
    Elementary—Activity programs Juvenile literature.
    [1. English language.   2. Literary recreations.]   I. Kenda,
    William.   II. Title.
LB1139.L3K45      1999
372.6—dc21                                      99-28053
                                                   CIP

PRINTED IN THE UNITED STATES OF AMERICA
9 8 7 6 5 4 3 2 1

# CONTENTS

POETRY CAN BE
VERY MOOOO-VING

# BE A WORD WIZARD

***P*erhaps** you like jokes, puzzles, games, stories, poems, or broadcasting—all ways to use words. It doesn't matter which you like best.

In this book, what does matter is that you have fun with them. Look on any page and you'll see something fun to do, and maybe more fun than you think.

If you like telling jokes, you'll see dozens of ways to do that. And you'll also see how jokes are put together, so you can get really good at making people laugh. Then you'll see how to go even further, by organizing your own Comedy Club and putting on a show.

If you like to make up stories or do puzzles, you'll see how to write a Japanese poem, invent apt new English words, and build a mysterious slot machine that runs entirely on words.

And everywhere you look, you'll also see little sections called **Word Wizardry.** Check out a few. You might see the longest word that has ever appeared on a map of the United States, learn how to use English halfway around the world, or find an Internet site that will show you exactly what's going on today in Hong Kong.

Check around enough and you'll see that the whole point of this book is to help you become a Word Wizard. The more you know about words and how they work, the more ways you can use them every day. Many times, that will be just for fun. Other times, it will be to understand unusual, complicated ideas.

Word Wizards know how to do both. So can you.

# FOR
# PARENTS
# AND TEACHERS

*M*ore than anything, kids need language. It's the base for all the other knowledge they will accumulate. It's the tool they'll use all their lives to discover what's true and what isn't.

Language gives kids the power to get a grip on new ideas and old ones, see into the details that do make a difference, and build the confidence to deal with whatever the world presents.

So for kids and parents, maybe the "job" of developing a sense of language isn't literally a job. It's much more like channeling a natural impulse. Kids want to learn, and they will.

What they learn will depend simply on how much they're shown, how they're treated, and how much time they spend in everyday atmospheres in which ideas matter.

1. **Set an example.** The more often a kid sees you reading, the likelier you'll hear "What's that? Can I see it?" Kids want to poke into parents' lives. Show them the book, the article, or the screen you're using, plus a detail or two that *you* find interesting.

2. **Tell real stories.** Kids already know how the manufactured stories of TV, movies, and books feel. Tell them about something unusual you saw yesterday, or something a relative once did. Ask *them* what their friends are doing, particularly if you know one or two well enough to get into detail.

3. **Talk up, not down.** Plain, straightforward English is a wonderful instrument. Dumbed-down or patronizing versions of it hardly ever work as well. If you want a child to see the

essence in a situation, talk about it seriously, in the same plain way you would with an adult.

4. **Share laughs.** Recognize that children are sharp observers, with what seems to be an inborn sense of the ridiculous. Cater to it. Have some fun with how oddly things are going in the family and the neighborhood.

5. *Use* **computers.** At worst, a kid's home or school PC can turn into a passive, isolating, and highly peculiar form of TV. At best, it can become a direct pathway into countless new ideas not visible in any other way.

6. **Make things.** Show kids how to use hand tools. Tools teach logic, precision, and control.

7. **Try other languages.** If no second language is usually spoken at home or in the neighborhood, make sure kids meet people who do speak something other than English. Learning even a little in a foreign language stretches a kid's ability with English.

8. **If you teach, teach language all the time.** Language enables science, mathematics, and everything else in the curriculum. Help your kids use language precisely, no matter what the "subject" is.

In short, make sure that kids get every possible encouragement to see the utility and the fun in language.

That's what we've tried to do in *Word Wizardry.*

For parents who might be concerned about a young person's reluctance to read or write beyond assigned homework, we hope that *Word Wizardry* will help. We've taken the most kid-attractive approach possible, inviting readers to write punch lines for cartoons, experiment with broadcasting, design original word games, write haiku, research family names, and practice stand-up comedy, all to encourage an enthusiasm for language.

Doing these projects also means that young people spend time looking into the finer details of language, learning to notice the subtleties in English spelling, diction, usage, and meaning. A sharper feeling for English results, and with it, we hope, the interest and confidence to keep on learning a little more each day.

For classroom teachers, the sheer variety built into *Word Wizardry* projects should also prove useful. While most of the projects are designed for a single student, others call for groups of three or four or an entire class.

We have also built in a considerable number of cross-learning situations. On page 208, for instance, the "See What's Behind Your Town's Name" project ties together language, oral history, local history, and speech. On page 103, there's "Help People Get Un-Lost," which combines language with local geography, surveying, math, and graphic art.

Our approach throughout *Word Wizardry* is to give readers a series of surprising experiences with language, all designed to encourage detailed, concentrated attention. We've also done what we can to accommodate a wide range of abilities, so that some children can enjoy a project like "Get Started as a Puzzlemaster" on page 118 while others "Square Up a Word Square" in the same chapter.

Computer work appears in *Word Wizardry,* too, including a variety of Internet-based projects. PCs and network connections now appear in so many homes and schools that "being a citizen of the wired world" is already a reality for many North American children. But impressive as it is, the growth of computer-based resources doesn't fundamentally change what children need to grasp to be successful in the actual world.

They need to get a good, solid, early, enthusiastic, and entertaining feeling for language. Growth will follow.

# 1. PLAY NAME GAMES

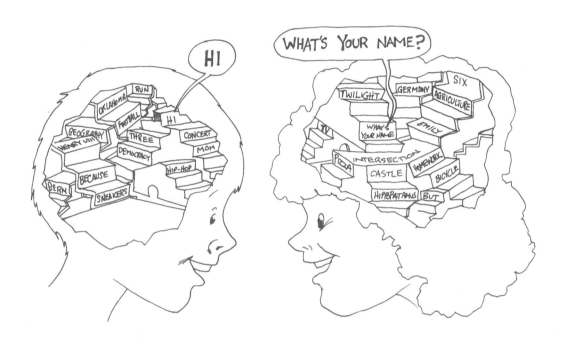

*H*ow do you know what to say? How does *anyone* know what to say?

It's a miracle, every time you use a word. You say it, read it, or hear it and somehow your brain keeps everything straight, so that the right idea just pops up automatically.

Unless you want to make a really stupid joke, there's no way you're going to say that "Mom" is your name. You won't say "apartment" either, because your sense of how to use words is so strong that wrong ones don't even surface.

That sense of language organizes the world for you. It helps you understand what's going on and how to respond, and it's at work constantly, attaching words and ideas to everything you come across. Just for a minute, try to imagine how it would feel to have no words at all for the things around you. What would that be like, with no automatic way to think or talk about the world?

You wouldn't know what to do about anything. Other people, weather, noises, smells, and a trillion other experiences would all be there, but not in the understandable patterns that words seem to give them. Your life would be constant confusion, with no easy way to learn how to act.

You'd need words and ideas, badly. That's why building a sense of language is one of the deepest impulses human beings feel. Everything around us has to be learned, so that we can live with it, fit it into sensible patterns, and understand what to do.

Having a word for "bicycle" gives it a label, so that you can remember it, think about it anytime you want, always see a clear mental picture of a two-wheeler, and always know that it's for riding, not for eating, playing music on, or calling "Mom." The word *bicycle* somehow says "bicycle" to you, and there's no chance you're going to be confused.

· · · · · · · ·
# PICTURE A NAME
· · · · · · · · · · · · · · · · · · · · ·

**W**rite down any two words you want.

—————————————

—————————————

Look back at the first one. If you wanted, could you draw a picture of it? Do you know the picture so well that you could add plenty of details? How long have you known about the thing in the picture? Does it remind you of other words or pictures?

And one more question: What does it have to do with the second word?

If you're like most people, your first word was probably a noun, the name of some person, place, or real thing. And it may not have too much to do with the second word. Both seem so clear to you and so different because you've used them thousands of times.

Now imagine how it would be to keep on with this list, adding hundreds and hundreds of words you know. Besides getting sore fingers, what do you think would happen? Would you ever come to an end, where you'd be absolutely convinced that you'd run out of words?

Probably not, because the supply of words and ideas you have comes from everything you've ever done, seen, felt, heard, read, thought, or guessed. It also comes from everything learned by the many generations

· · · · · · · ·
# PICTURE A NAME
## *continued*

of people who've preceded you. Words and ideas are the way everyone has made sense out of the world, forever. The meanings inside them have changed, grown, and regrown for centuries, sometimes in strange and unpredictable ways, but generally to create clearer and better ways to communicate.

Words are names. They identify everything and everybody, and always have, in thousands of different languages.

### WORD WIZARDRY

Visit beautiful Lake Webster. It used to be called Chargoggaoggmanchaugagoggchaubunagungamaugg.

. . . . . . . .
# WHERE'S MY NAME?
. . . . . . . . . . . . . . . . . . . .

**T**hink about your own name. The original source for it isn't too likely to be Nipmuc, a tribal language that was last spoken about 300 years ago in Massachusetts and the other New England states. It's much more likely to be English, Spanish, or one of the other major languages brought to North America by the millions who began to settle here after 1650.

Your family probably had five or six reasons they chose your name. The language they speak was the most important, but so were names already in the family, plus some combination of the family's history, religion, hopes, and sense of style. Parents usually put serious thought into choosing a child's name, and see a whole set of meanings in it.

Even if you've heard already, ask your family again why they chose your name. What you'll probably get is a long explanation, not a short one, and you can use it to look a little more deeply into your name.

The ten most popular names today:

| *Girls* | *Boys* |
|---------|--------|
| Brittany | Michael |
| Ashley | Christopher |
| Jessica | Matthew |
| Amanda | Joshua |
| Sarah | Andrew |
| Megan | James |
| Caitlin | John |
| Samantha | Nicholas |
| Stephanie | Justin |
| Katherine | David |

Maybe your name is on the "popular" list, and maybe not. That doesn't matter so much, because all first names are loaded with meanings that make them special.

Some names, like Sarah, have been used for so long that they've built up histories of their own. Sarah is originally an ancient Hebrew name, meaning "princess." It's a name so attractive that it's been taken into other languages over the centuries.

Nicholas comes from Greek, where it means "victory of the people," and has also been used in other European languages as a saint's name for almost 2,000 years.

· · · · · · · ·
# WHERE'S MY NAME?
## *continued*

So most parents usually think of names like Sarah and Nicholas as "traditional," or belonging to a stock of names popular in English for centuries. Choosing one of them indicates that a positive set of meanings comes along, especially if the name sounds good with the family name, has other connections with the family's own history, and is currently in style.

But that's not a guarantee. Pure style is the most important factor to some parents, whereas others feel that they should use only names already in the family. Still others, such as some African-American and West Indian parents, like unique names, so that their children will be unlikely to meet others who have the same name.

With so many reasons for choosing names, it's not easy to see exactly what's behind any one name, even your own. But you can clear up at least some of the mysteries.

Here's how.

# GET INSIDE YOUR OWN NAME

To check out your first name, remember everything your family has told you about why they chose it. Then have a look at the six questions below. No matter how you answer them, you'll get deeper into the background of your own name and also learn a system that will enable you to start analyzing anybody's name.

### Here's what you need:

*A pencil and some scrap paper, for making notes*

*Some friends who might like to know more about their names*

### Here's what you do:

1. Start by answering "Y" or "N" to the first question. Then follow the directions to see which one to answer next.

   *1.* Do you know people with the same first name as yours?

   Y—go to 2.   N—go to 6.

   *2.* Is your first name "traditional"? Has it been given to children for a long time, either in English or in other languages?

   Y—go to 3.   N—go to 6.

   *3.* Do you know if famous saints, prophets, kings, queens, or heroes from the past had your first name?

   Y—go to 4.   N—go to 6.

   *4.* Do you know how your first name is spelled and pronounced in some other languages?

   Y—go to 5.   N—go to 6.

   *5.* If you said yes to the last question, write down your name in English and in the other languages. Split it into pieces in all the languages, based on how it sounds.

| | *English* | *French* | *German* | *Italian* | *Other* |
|---|---|---|---|---|---|
| Example: | Wil-liam | Guil-laume | Wil-helm | Gug-li-el-mo | |
| Your name: | _____ | _____ | _____ | _____ | _____ |

· · · · · · · ·
# GET INSIDE YOUR OWN NAME
## *continued*

**6.** Do you see your name—or parts of it—in the lists below? Look closely, because even though you may not find a perfect match, you might see a piece or two that sounds or looks like a syllable in your name.

Mark whatever comes close. Then look at the English meanings next to the names, which all come originally from a variety of ancient languages. It may turn out that your own name is close to one of them, so that it suggests "peace," "pearl," or something else that's always been admired. Or maybe there's no match at all, because your name is so unusual.

| Boys' Names | English Meanings | Original Language |
| --- | --- | --- |
| Alexander | Defender of men | Greek |
| Benjamin | The right hand | Hebrew |
| Charles | A man | Old German |
| Chiang | Strong | Chinese |
| Edward | Happy guardian | Old English |
| Francis | A Frenchman | Latin |
| Geoffrey | Peace | Norman |
| George | Farmer | Greek |
| Hashim | Generous | Arabic |
| Jamal | Handsome | Arabic |
| John | God has favored | Hebrew |
| Lewis | Famous fighter | Old German |
| Patrick | A nobleman | Latin |
| Rashid | Righteous | Arabic |
| Richard | Stern ruler | Norman |
| Thomas | Twin | Aramaic |
| William | Well helmeted | Old German |
| Zhi | Ambitious | Chinese |

| Girls' Names | English Meanings | Original Language |
| --- | --- | --- |
| Alice | Nobility | Old German |
| Ann | God has favored me | Hebrew |
| Carol | A woman | Old German |
| Elizabeth | Fullness of God | Hebrew |

# GET INSIDE YOUR OWN NAME
## *continued*

| | | |
|---|---|---|
| Farah | Cheerful | Arabic |
| Felicia | Happiness | Latin |
| Jane | God has favored | Hebrew |
| Katherine | Pure | Greek |
| Malikah | Queen | Arabic |
| Margaret | Pearl | Greek |
| Mary | Lady | Hebrew |
| Mei | Beautiful | Chinese |
| Rashida | Pious | Arabic |
| Renee | Reborn | French |
| Susan | Lily | Hebrew |
| Tanisha | Born on a Monday | Hausa |
| Virginia | Queen | Latin |
| Xia | Cloud | Chinese |

2. Look back at all your answers and marks. They won't tell you everything about your name, but you'll see that a basic system of history, meaning, and sound lies behind almost every possible name.

Try out the yes-or-no questions and the list with some of your friends' names, or with names in your family. People are always interested in the qualities that their names suggest, and they'll be amazed by how much you can show them.

**WORD WIZARDRY**

**NAMES OF FOUR ACTUAL PEOPLE:**

Gaston J. Feeblebunny
Preserved Fish, Jr.
Daphne Reader's Digest Taione
Halloween Buggage

# CREATE YOUR OWN WORDS

**I**f you tried the names system, maybe you've already guessed that something like it could work for every word in English. Like names, all words have major and minor meanings to them, and many of those come from deep in the past or from other languages. In fact, modern English now includes so many words and ideas built up from so many sources that it's full of surprises.

When you say "bicycle," you're actually speaking a modern English version of some combined Latin and Greek from more than 2,000 years ago. The "bi" part of the word means "two" in Latin, and "cycle" comes from the ancient Greek for "circle" or "wheel." Put them together and you get a two-wheeler. And you don't get a *unicycle*, because "uni" means "one" in Latin. Or a *tricycle*, because "tri" means "three."

And when you say "bike," you're still using Latin and Greek, just jamming them together to make a shorter, simpler word for the same idea. Every language works like that, slowly building new words out of old ones and matching them up to new ideas. To see how that works and have a little fun with it, check this out.

Imagine that the weird-looking thing on the table is a new invention of yours, a toy that you've designed for two-year-olds. It's made out of something like modeling clay, so that little kids can squeeze it and reshape it any way they want. But it always returns to looking like a dog after they put it down. It can't be torn into pieces, and it's even safe to chew on.

· · · · · · · ·
# CREATE YOUR OWN WORDS
### *continued*

It's a great invention, never seen before. All you need now is a name for it, so that parents will understand that your toy is unique, fun, safe, and definitely something a two-year-old would love.

What do you call it? Magic Dog? That's not bad, but maybe it isn't the best way to help people understand what's so unusual about your toy. With just a word or two, you need to get their attention, create a clear picture of what the toy does, and make sure that the name you invent for it sounds so good that it will be easy to remember. Try it.

### *Here's what you need:*
*A pencil, and a pen that writes in any color other than gray*

*Some scrap paper to try out your ideas*

### *Here's what you do:*

**1.** Think about the idea behind the toy. Look at the left side of this list and use your pencil to write in some more words that clearly describe what the toy is.

Then work on the right side, with your pen. Write in some words that show how the toy works. Don't try for the perfect name yet.

# CREATE YOUR OWN WORDS

## *continued*

### The Toy

| *Is* | *Works By* |
|------|-----------|
| animal | squeezing |
| clay | changing shape |
| ———— | ————— |
| ———— | ————— |
| ———— | ————— |
| ———— | ————— |

**2.** Once you have the two lists, mark the words that also suggest how different the toy is.

**3.** Now think about the toy as a picture. Look at both lists, and think up some new words that describe exactly what it looks like. Use your pen, and add the new words to this list:

### Looks

| lumpy | smooth |
|-------|--------|
| ———— | ———— |
| ———— | ———— |
| ———— | ———— |
| ———— | ———— |

**4.** Mark the one or two that seem clearest to you, then use your scrap paper to put them together with the words you marked from the first two lists.

See if there are ways the words could combine, so that what the toy is, how it looks, and what it does come clear all at once. Think about both the pen and the pencil words.

**5.** Now comes the fun part. Look back over all the words you have and try out some new thinking.

Is there one single word that is good enough to do the job as the toy's name, or do you need two? Are there some words that didn't even occur to you at first now showing up on the scrap paper? Is this toy maybe Blobby Dog, or Squeezit?

Keep going until you get something you really like. But remember: You're inventing a totally new word for a toy, so you need something that's unique, attractive, clear, and good-sounding. Good words always have some music to them.

Say your best ideas out loud a few times before picking the winner. Then make it a piece of Word Wizardry, because it is.

**WORD WIZARDRY**

**THE TOY'S NAME IS:**

———————————

## ·······
# TRY OUT SNEAKY WORD GAMES
·····················

**I**f English were perfectly logical, which it isn't, you'd never have a second's trouble figuring out how words should be spelled or pronounced. Every letter would stand for exactly the same sound, and saying or spelling a new word would never be a problem.

But the language wouldn't be much fun, either. You'd have to do without all the mysterious words that fill up real English, like *foreign, parishioner,* and *onslaught.* There wouldn't be much feeling left in the language or as many ways to put together ideas, sounds, and looks to create unique words.

Real English has thousands of ways to do that, basically because it works like a code. There's an alphabet of 26 letters, plus a huge set of sounds, and the code for how they match up to make words has never been particularly simple. But there are some ways to poke into it, and if you try just one of them, you'll probably be surprised by how much of the code you and your friends have already cracked.

It's a game, and easy to set up for two, three, or four players.

. . . . . . . .
# TRY OUT SNEAKY WORD GAMES
## *continued*

### *Here's what you need:*

*A watch that shows minutes and seconds*

*A pencil and some paper for each player*

### *Here's what you do:*

1. Start by having everybody say these words out loud. Notice that they're all a bit sneaky.

   They look alike but don't sound alike, and they all mean something different.

   | Code | Sound |
   |------|-------|
   | tough | tuff |
   | thought | thawt |
   | through | thru |
   | trough | troff |
   | bough | bau |
   | dough | doe |
   | drought | drowt |

2. Then make a scorecard for each player, with one column on it headed "Code" and the other "Sound."

3. Tell everybody to look back at the list of words you've just read aloud, because the point of this game is to think up strange words in a hurry. Each player has to fill up both sides of the scorecard, starting with "Code."

   You do this by taking turns and using the watch.

   Tell the first player how to start. The challenge is to write down six real words that fit the "Code" column because they absolutely *don't* look like they sound.

4. When the player is ready to go, check the watch to see how long it will take to get the words down. Mark the total time on the player's card, then give each of the others a turn.

5. Now look at the "Sound" column, where the players need to fill in real words that are spelled *exactly* like they sound.

   Tell everybody that this part can actually be hard, so all they need is five words.

   Then take turns again, and write down the time each player needs.

6. When everybody's done, look at all the times. The winner is the player with the shortest times between the "Code" and the "Sound."

. . . . . . . .

# TRY OUT SNEAKY WORD GAMES

## *continued*

Why play with the differences? Because people who are really good with English words have a feeling for how they look and sound. Knowing both is important, because modern English has been built up from so many old and new sources that it's a deeply complicated mixture. Spellings can come partly from Greek, Latin, German—even from an old mathematician's idea of how spoken Arabic ought to look in English. That's how algebra got taken into English as a word.

### WORD WIZARDRY

#### WORDS FROM DEEP IN THE CODE:

*abracadabra,* a word good for casting a magic spell or any other sort of make-believe

*mulligatawny,* a word for an East Indian soup, especially good if you like curry

*ox,* a word for a big animal, in the same class as cows and often very hardworking

*persnickety,* a word that describes someone who is much too fussy and a lot too particular

........
# FIND OUT WHAT'S BETTER THAN "AWESOME"

. . . . . . . . . . . . . . . . . . .

**N**o matter how you did with Code and Sound, you probably saw right away that English words can be perfect for all sorts of games. People have made crossword puzzles and board games out of them for centuries, but not every word game needs to happen on paper.

Think about words like *awesome* or *phat.* You hear them dozens of times every day, but usually without an exact meaning attached. Depending on the situation, either one can mean "beautiful," "fun," "I really want to do that," "special," "yes," or maybe even "disgusting."

To have some fun with that, imagine how "awesome" must have gotten started. No books or dictionaries ever defined it as such an all-purpose word, but for some reason people began to use it more and more in conversation. The word just grew, and if you'd like to see how quickly and unpredictably that can happen, here's a game you can try at school.

The point is to see how long it takes to make a totally new word popular.

## . . . . . . . .
# FIND OUT WHAT'S BETTER THAN "AWESOME"
### *continued*

**Here's what you need:**

*Two friends who'd like to help you out*

*A week at school, with all three of you agreeing to use a new word as often as possible*

**Here's what you do:**

1.  Ask the two friends whether they think "awesome" could use some improvement. Show them this list of other, older words that once had the same general meaning as "awesome."

    | | | |
    |---|---|---|
    | keen | cool | nifty |
    | super | fantastic | sharp |
    | bad | wild | terrific |
    | monster | neat | perfect |

    If they like one of those, mark it.

2.  Then ask them to think about "awesome" in a different way. What if you all tried to invent a way of saying *how* awesome something is? Are there single words that could fit in these blanks?

    much better than awesome
    _____

    somewhat better than awesome
    _____

    not quite awesome
    _____

    way beneath awesome
    _____

    no chance to be awesome
    _____

3.  Spend some time on both #1 and #2, because what you're trying to do is zero in on a word that strikes you as unique and new. Try out all your new-word ideas by saying them as part of sentences, to see how easy and natural each one sounds.

4.  Now pick the winner. It doesn't matter whether it's from your work on #1 or #2, but it should have a sound and a feeling that you think most people would like right away.

5.  Then work out a plan for starting to use the word at school. Every time each of you would otherwise say "awesome" to people, say the new word instead. You'll probably get some funny looks at first, but if the three of you keep at it for a couple of days, it won't be long before you start hearing other people use the word.

· · · · · · · ·
# FIND OUT WHAT'S BETTER THAN "AWESOME"
## *continued*

If your new word is good enough, maybe you'll even start a trend. Nobody knows who started "awesome," but if your word starts moving from friends to classmates to people at other schools, you'll know exactly who started it.

**WORD WIZARDRY**

**NEW WORDS TRAVEL:**

| *from* | *to* |
| --- | --- |
| young people | older people |
| small groups | bigger groups |
| big towns | smaller towns |

........

# SPIN THE WORD WHEEL OF CHANCE

. . . . . . . . . . . . . . . . . . . .

**I**f a party is coming up, people will generally want to have an organized game or two ready. But which kind is always a problem, because most games you buy can be too easy for some players and too hard for others. And some games just take too long.

One way around that is to try "Word Wheel of Chance," a simple word game you can make and set up yourself. The game runs on pure chance, so people of any age can play without having to know too many rules. It goes quickly, too, with each player's turn taking just a few seconds.

Have a look at how to put it together.

### Here's what you need:

*Black felt-tipped pen*

*Three paper plates*

*Scissors*

*One small sheet of thick, colored construction paper*

*Ruler*

*Three two-pronged paper fasteners*

*A drawing compass with a point strong enough to poke holes in the construction paper*

*Pencils and small sheets of paper, for the players to use during the game*

### Here's what you do:

1. Look at the drawing. Then use the pen to copy exactly those letters around the edges of all three paper plates. The letters don't make a complete alphabet, but arranging them that way will make the finished game quicker to play.

2. Cut three skinny rectangles out of the construction paper. They should be about 1/2 inch (1.3 centimeters) high, and slightly longer than half of your plates' diameter.

   Then measure in about 3/4 inch (2 centimeters) from the short edge of each rectangle. Make a mark halfway along those lines, then carefully use the compass to poke a hole through the mark.

3. Get one fastener to see if its set of prongs will fit through one of the holes. If it won't, work the compass point gently around the edges of all three holes until you enlarge them just enough to make a good fit, so the prongs will turn easily in the holes.

   Then do the same to all three plates, with the holes exactly in their centers.

4. Cut pointed ends on each rectangle, and use the fasteners to connect them to the plates. Be careful when you spread the prongs, because you can't have

· · · · · · · ·
# Spin the Word Wheel of Chance
## *continued*

the final fit too tight. Test each pointer to see that it spins well.

**5.** Once everything is together, all you need is players.

Put one or more of the plates on a table, and tell the players the rules. All they have to do is spin the pointer, write down the letter it lands on, and give the next player a turn to do the same. The first player to get enough letters to make a six-letter word wins.

When you play, you'll all see some interesting patterns develop. One is that everyone will be after the vowels *a, e, i, o,* and *u,* because you can't make real words without them. If one player gets *e* several times, you may even hear someone asking to trade letters.

Another pattern will be how often each player has to rethink what could be done with a given collection of letters. Random chance may be running the game, but making sense is what wins it.

### Word Wizardry

*Qwerty* is a good six-letter word that describes how keyboards are laid out. When manual typewriters were invented, the idea was to make the most often used letters hard to reach, so that typists wouldn't type too fast. That would jam the machines' keys. Look at the top row on your own keyboard.

· · · · · · · ·
# SEE INTO THE HISTORY OF FAMILY NAMES
· · · · · · · · · · · · · · · · · · · ·

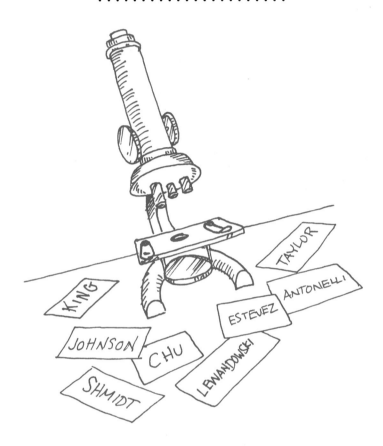

Suppose that 50 years from now, someone actually invents a Word Microscope. It's a device so powerful that it reveals everything about every word in English. It can even see all the way down into family names, including your own.

But to do its work on your family name, the Word Microscope will need a little help getting focused. That's because every family's history is unique, with a long string of marriages, moves, and language changes all combining to build it. To use the Word Microscope, you'll need to clarify at least some of your family's background before reaching for the knobs.

········
# SEE INTO THE HISTORY OF FAMILY NAMES
## *continued*

### *Here's what you need:*

*One talk each with three different adult relatives, to get their stories about your family's history*

*A supply of graph paper, a pencil, and a ruler, to make some charts*

### *Here's what you do:*

1. Tell a parent that you'd like to do an interview soon on three subjects:

   • Who were the parent's own grandparents? When and where did they live?

   • How many children did those grandparents have? Whom did the children marry, and what new last names began to be used at that time?

   • Did any of those people grow up speaking some language other than English? Did any of their last names change through remarriages, or for any other reason?

2. To get ready for that talk, get out one sheet of graph paper and make a horizontal chart that looks like the one below. When you're done, make three more just like it, two to use when you interview your other two relatives and one for a final copy.

Our Family Names

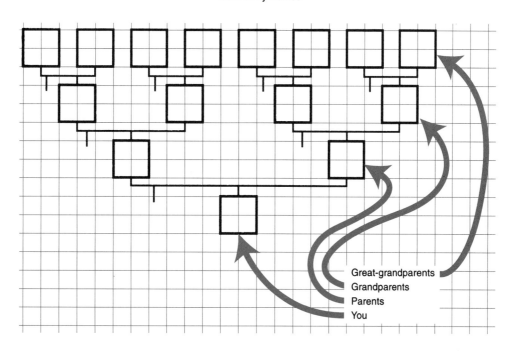

Great-grandparents
Grandparents
Parents
You

........

# SEE INTO THE HISTORY OF FAMILY NAMES
## *continued*

3. When you interview your parent, use the chart to help with getting your three questions answered. Write the names you're told into the rows of boxes, with one row devoted to each generation of people, right down to the row that includes you.

   Along the way, draw in additional boxes if you need them, and use the space around all boxes to note down why any family-name changes happened.

   Be sure to ask about marriages, remarriages, and moves from one country to another, and don't forget to ask which languages the people used. Fill in everything you can.

4. Take your filled-in chart and one blank one when you interview the second relative. Show that person what you have so far, and use the blank chart to make notes on any changes or additions you get. Do the same with the third relative.

5. Then sit down with all three charts, to combine everything you've learned. Use your last blank chart to make a neat, organized, final copy.

At this point, what you'll already have is a family tree, and everybody who helped you will want to see it. You may find that your final copy makes them think of even more family stories.

If you then tell everybody that there are ways to see even deeper into the family name, they'll definitely be interested. That's your chance to go to the Word Microscope, where at least one of the names your family has used will probably snap into focus.

Here are the kinds of details you'll see. Check through them. You probably won't find your exact family name, but you may well see a basic piece of it here.

### *Meaning of Many Family Names = "Son Of"*

| Language/ Nationality | "Son Of" | Sample Names | Meaning |
|---|---|---|---|
| Irish | O' | O'Hara | Son of Henry |
| Scottish | Mc, Mac | McPherson | Son of the parson |
| Welsh | ap | Powell (apHowell) | Son of Howell |
| Spanish | ez | Alvarez | Son of Alva |
| Greek | poulos | Theodoropoulos | Son of Theodore |

. . . . . . . .
# SEE INTO THE HISTORY OF FAMILY NAMES
## *continued*

| Hebrew | ben | ben Ezra | Son of Ezra |
| Portuguese | es | Gomes | Son of Gomo |
| Scandinavian | sen | Jensen | Son of John |
| Slavic | ov | Ivanov | Son of Ivan (John) |
| Slavic | vic | Petrovic | Son of Peter |
| Slavic | wicz | Rabinowicz | Son of the rabbi |

### *Source of Thousands of Family Names = Three First Names*

| From John | | From Robert | | From Richard | |
|---|---|---|---|---|---|
| Jones | Janik | Robinson | Dobbs | Dixon | Hickox |
| Jennings | Hancock | Hopkins | Hodge | Rich | Riccardo |
| Hansen | Jensen | Rutgers | Ruggiero | Pritchard | Ricketts |
| Giovanitti | Johnson | Roberge | Robertson | Richards | Richardson |

### *Four Most Common Names in the World = Li, Wang, Smith, Jones*

In fact, the world is so full of "Smiths" that there are at least 12 basic versions of the name, each one based on the original words for "blacksmith" in a variety of languages. Check these out.

| | | |
|---|---|---|
| Schmidt | Smidnovic | Kovacs |
| Schmitz | Sippanen | Fevre |
| Smed | Kowalski | Kalvaitis |
| Schmieder | Kuznets | McGowan |

Then there's "Jim Smith," a full name so common in the United States that there's even a Jim Smith Club, with thousands of members. Every summer, they organize baseball games just to set up situations where every single player, umpire, and spectator is named Jim Smith.

· · · · · · · ·

# SEE INTO THE HISTORY OF FAMILY NAMES
## *continued*

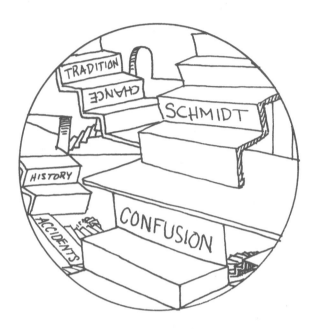

Look deep into the Word Microscope. Perhaps you'll see many mysterious factors that have been at work to shape your name. You've come from countless ancestors, almost all of them from somewhere else in the world. Those people spoke different languages, moved from country to country, married, changed their own names, selected new names for their children, followed fashions in names, and kept on doing all of that for generations.

So right now, you might say that your name has really come not from somewhere, but from everywhere. All names slowly get built that way, just like all the other words you know. They've risen up through history toward you—for every reason from religious tradition to random chance—to help identify who you are.

### WORD WIZARDRY

President Franklin Delano Roosevelt had two seventeenth-century European ancestors: the Dutchman Claes Martenzen van *Rosenvelt* and the Frenchman Philippe *de la Noye*.

Paul Revere's father was named Apollos de *Revoire*.

# 2. Design Your Own Jokes and Cartoons

**W**hat's the best cartoon you've ever seen, and why did it make you laugh? Was it just the drawing, just the words, or both at once?

Probably it was both, because good cartoons combine words and art to create the joke. No matter how weird a dinosaur and a computer might look together, there's no joke in the cartoon until some words get added. Maybe the dinosaur says:

> "www.extinct.com?"
> or "Me 50 tons, you 14 pounds. Me win."
> or "Hi. How did you like my movie?"

The words finish the joke. You see them, make an instant connection with the drawing, and get the point. You also get a joke you can repeat, because the words will organize the way you describe the cartoon to somebody else.

Good cartoonists know that, and they try to match art and words as closely as they can. But they also know that no two people have exactly the same sense of humor, so they don't make the connection too tight. Like good jokes, good cartoons need to be open, with a little bit left for people to imagine.

· · · · · · · ·
# TRY OUT CARTOONING
· · · · · · · · · · · · · · · · · · · ·

**H**ere's how to try a cartoon of your own. Even if you don't think you're very good at drawing, you already do know how to think up good cartoons.

### Here's what you need:

*A pencil and some sketch paper*

*A dozen small scraps of paper*

### Here's what you do:

1. Think about the kinds of cartoons you and your friends like. Are they about school, or maybe about animals, parents, sports, outer space, or something special going on where you live?

2. If a good idea comes to you right away, sketch it out as fast as you can, without worrying about making your art look perfect. Just get the idea down, even if it looks only like a blob or two on the page. Then think some more, because getting one idea started will probably make you think of two or three more. Sketch them, too, as fast as you can.

3. Now it's time to slow down. Put a scrap of paper next to the first sketch you did, look at the sketch for a bit, and imagine exactly what could be going on there. If the blobs are people, one could be saying something ridiculous to the other. If you see an animal or two, maybe they could be talking, using a vending machine, or doing

something else that real animals can't do.

Imagine how the cartoon *sounds,* because it does have a sound hiding in it, and that's what completes the joke.

When a funny line occurs to you, write it down on one of the scraps and put it next to the sketch. If you think of more, write them down, too.

4. Then do something really weird. Move one of your funny lines next to one of the other sketches you made.

Could it work there, and be funny for a completely different reason? Or does it make you think of a whole new idea for both art and words?

· · · · · · · ·
# TRY OUT CARTOONING
## *continued*

**5.** Keep going until one of two things happens. You may come up with one cartoon idea so good that you want to finish the art, write in the funny line, and show it to people.

Or you may have a number of ideas, all promising. If that happens, put your work away and come back to it in a day or two. Like magic, one of those ideas will probably seem completely changed to you, and you may suddenly have a terrific cartoon.

It's strange, but cartoons, poems, jokes, and stories sometimes develop that way. After you get them started, they can take on lives of their own and work away in your memory, turning into something completely new.

### WORD WIZARDRY

Some cartoon characters speak a strange language. When they get mad, they say, "*!#!!@!!"

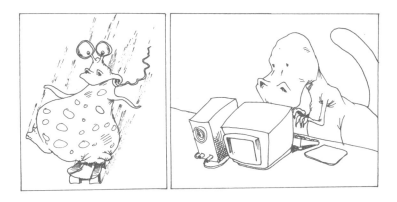

# KNOW IT: YOU'RE A POET

You are a poet, whether you know it or not.

By your age, you've seen and heard thousands of poems, in everything from song lyrics and hymns to schoolbooks, jokes, and verses in the Bible, Koran, or Torah. Poetic language is all around you, sometimes serious and other times silly, but always so perfect in its way that it strikes you right away. You can't help paying attention.

One reason is how poetic language sounds. It's really music, with the pure sound of each word just as important as what the word means. Sometimes the sound is even more important.

Listen to this:

> I once had a friend named O'Brien,
> World-famous for screaming and crying.

Those two lines are silly, but if you read them aloud, they do roll along in a deliberate way. There's a beat to them, and a rhyme at the end that makes a joke. You may even get the feeling that there could be more to say about O'Brien, because the two lines set up a story that doesn't sound finished.

See what you can do to finish it.

You're a poet,
And don't know it.
But your feet show
They're Longfellows.

### Here's what you need:

*A pencil and a few full-size sheets of lined paper*

*Fifteen minutes one day to think up a finish, and fifteen the next to improve it or figure out something completely different*

### Here's what you do:

**1.** Copy the first two lines about O'Brien on the top of a page. Then copy these lines right under them.

You could _____ him all _____,
From _____ to _____,
Even if _____ _____ _____ trying.

**2.** Think about the blanks. Could you *hear* him all *day*? Or all *night,* all *week,* or all *over*?

Pick one, and then think about the next line. Can you make it rhyme at the end, maybe by using *L.A.*? Or *the Heights, Pikes Peak,* or *supernovas*?

Spend a few minutes trying different words in the blanks.

· · · · · · · ·

# KNOW IT: YOU'RE A POET

## *continued*

You'll be surprised by what happens, because strange ideas will start to occur to you, probably better than these two.

*You could hear him all day
From New York to L.A.*

*You could hear him all week
From here to Pikes Peak*

3. Then read your ideas aloud a few times, for two reasons. You want them to have the right beat as a pair of lines, and you want them to lead into the fifth line that ends the joke.

   When you have something good, get a fresh piece of paper. Recopy the first two lines about O'Brien, add your two, and read all four aloud several times. That will start to give you a feeling about what the fifth line could say.

4. On that page, write down all the ideas you get for the fifth line. Some could be about O'Brien himself. Others could be about what happened because of all his noise. Try a few like these.

*Even when he wasn't much
trying.*

*So loud your ears would start
frying.*

You can also change the whole situation, by using a completely different last line that still rhymes fairly closely with *crying*. That creates a new kind of joke. Try the first four lines you already have with closings like these.

*Wailing away like a fire-truck
siren.*

*Filling the sky with people sent
flying.*

Whatever you decide, read all five lines aloud when you're done. You'll have the short, joking kind of poem called a limerick, and maybe you'll want to try a few others. Here's a start.

*I once had an aunt named
Miranda
Whose cat was as big as a panda
There's no school like our school,
Never quite empty and never
quite full*

### WORD WIZARDRY

Limerick is a city in Ireland. These jokes are named after it.

# PUT ON A SHOW AT THE COMEDY CLUB

If you and your friends like telling jokes, here's a way to turn it into even more fun. Think about putting on a comedy show, with each friend taking a turn in the spotlight. You could even organize it as a Comedy Club.

Unless you have big ambitions, you needn't worry about having a real stage, a working spotlight, or anything else too complicated. All you need to start is three or four friends who'd like to perform, plus a quiet room where you can gather an audience.

To make the show a good one, though, you do need a big supply of clear, precise, interesting, easy, active, strong, inviting, logical, unusual, memorable, and altogether surprising words. Jokes don't work until you find the perfect words.

But you can work them out. All it takes is some rehearsal time with your friends.

········

# PUT ON A SHOW AT THE COMEDY CLUB

## *continued*

### *Here's what you need:*

*Several friends who'll agree that they'd like to tell jokes to an audience*

*Free time for all of you to rehearse together, probably two or three times*

*Scrap paper and pencils for everybody to use at the rehearsals*

### *Here's what you do:*

1. Get everybody together for a first rehearsal and distribute the paper and pencils. Ask each person to stand in front of the group and tell a favorite joke.

   Have everybody else listen closely, so that each person can quickly note down any ideas about how to improve the joke. Keep going until you've heard everybody's favorites.

2. Then talk over all the notes, because there will probably be two kinds. Some will be about jokes that seemed perfect right away, and that's good.

   But pay attention to the other notes. If one or two jokes seemed too long, too short, or just not funny enough, get the whole group to work on them.

3. Do it this way, by drawing and labeling three big boxes on a piece of paper.

| Basic Situation |
| --- |
| Odd Complication |
| Weird Result |

All jokes are different, of course, but many do work just like the set of boxes. They're little stories, and they need a clear way to get to the laugh line at the end.

Have the group brainstorm for a few minutes about each joke that needs to be improved, but stop as soon as you have something slightly better for the Complication or Result boxes.

Save any more group work for your next rehearsal, because everybody is likely to come back in a different mood, ready to work on new ideas.

4. Try all the jokes again at the second rehearsal, but do the brainstorming a different way, based on one question and three possible answers.

## *What's the Joke?*

| A Story | A Dialogue | A Situation |
| --- | --- | --- |
| The Comedian **OR** | The Comedian **OR** | The Comedian |
| Tells? | Repeats? | Acts Out? |

. . . . . . . .

# PUT ON A SHOW AT THE COMEDY CLUB
## *continued*

If a joke still seems weak, maybe it just needs to be moved from one box to another, so that the situation is presented in a different style. Brainstorm it. Big changes sometimes work far better than small ones.

5. When everybody's material is as good as the brainstorming can make it, ask your friends the real question: Are they ready to put on a show and invite people?

If they are, think about having just one more rehearsal, to ensure that each person feels confident about all the jokes.

Standing up in front of a group of people and making them laugh does take confidence. But if you're prepared and you know your jokes are set up just right, there's no other feeling like it.

### WORD WIZARDRY

Why is "quiz" a one-word joke? Because in 1780, James Daly made it up as a new word, and then hired people to spend a whole night scribbling it all over the streets and walls of Dublin. When everybody else saw it the next morning, all knew it was a joke. As time went on, they began to use the word *quiz* to mean a trick, a quick puzzle, a quick test, or a surprise test.

## DON'T BE CRUEL

That Jonathan, he's the ugliest kid in school.
So ugly the bus driver quit—she couldn't take it
anymore. Coach makes Jonathan play catcher,
so he has to wear a mask. Principal says, "Hey,
Jonathan, get down in the basement. That's where
we put your locker."

Unless you're Jonathan, you could think that jokes like these are funny. They're usually about somebody unpopular, and what they do is exaggerate how dumb, clumsy, skinny, fat, tall, short, or just plain unusual the kid seems to be.

But basically they're cruel. They wind up hurting, even if all they seem to do is use the kid's name as a way of getting off a nasty line.

The good part is that almost everybody learns somehow to avoid jokes that are too mean or too personal. Something like a built-in censor develops. We still tell jokes to point out absurd situations and get laughs, but not to be mean.

To see where the limits are, and how definite they are, all you need to do is watch a little TV.

### Here's what you need:
*A clear memory of the times people have laughed at you*
*A chance to watch your favorite TV sitcoms by yourself, so you can study them*
*Pencil and paper, to make charts while you watch*

### Here's what you do:

**1.** Watch a sitcom that's good, but isn't your favorite. While you do, try to notice what's used as the way to get laughs.

Is it simply who the characters are? Or is it also what they say and do?

## DON'T BE CRUEL

*continued*

Do they make dumb plans that don't work out? Do they misunderstand what's happening?

2. Whatever you think, turn off the show and make this simple chart before you watch anything more.

| Often | Never |
|-------|-------|
|       |       |
|       |       |
|       |       |
|       |       |
|       |       |
|       |       |

3. Then watch a show you like a little better, and fill in the "Often" column when you notice repeating situations that are used to get laughs. Is one character always trying to get a date and always failing? Or is another character constantly working on

stupid plans to get rich?

Are certain kids trying to act older than they are?

4. Once you have a few notes about "Often," take a look at the "Never" column of your chart and think about what the show *doesn't* use as a basis for laugh lines. That's harder, but if you start by writing in "race" and then "religion," you'll probably think of at least five or six more subjects that the show avoids completely. What about handicaps, retardation, or homelessness?

5. Then check out your favorite show. Its "Often" list is going to be both different from and better than the one you've made so far. But the "Never" list will probably be exactly the same.

That's because good comedy can't be seriously offensive, whether it's a TV show or just a joke you're telling to friends. When being mean starts, being funny stops.

### WORD WIZARDRY

Calling somebody a dunce isn't very nice, but maybe it should be. Today the word *dunce* means a stupid, ignorant person. Yet the word comes from the name of *Duns* Scotus, a brilliant thirteenth-century scholar, not stupid or ignorant at all. His ideas were so strong that they scared people, and anybody believing him was ridiculed. They were called Dunsmen, or dunces.

········
# MOMS AND DADS NEED LAUGHS, TOO
·····················

**I**f you've ever made special cards of your own for Mother's Day, Father's Day, or a parent's birthday, you know that they're always a big hit. Parents appreciate getting something personal, particularly when they can see the time and effort behind your design.

But think about how much more they'd like a card that's not just good-looking, but laid out unpredictably. What if you designed a card that looks like a comic strip, with your mother or father as the hero?

### Here's what you need:

*A pencil*

*Plenty of scrap paper*

*A set of colored pencils or markers*

*Two sheets of clean, full-size paper*

### Here's what you do:

1. Instead of just "Happy Birthday" or "Happy Mother's Day," think about a comic-strip kind of headline to use for your card. Maybe it could be something like:
   - Mom the Magnificent
   - The Totally Amazing Adventures of *Daring Dad*
   - Mom and Dad Save the World!!!

2. Once you have a rough idea for a title, go to your scrap paper right away and start thinking about pictures that might *exaggerate the daily good things* your parent does. Spend some time on this, because you want to end up with drawings that are not just fun, but also show that you really see into what your parent *does* every day. Think about it this way, with no limits on what you use as material.

| Real Situation | Exaggerated, Comic-Strip Version |
|---|---|
| Dad's good at fixing the car. | All four tires on the car are flat and smoke is coming out of the hood. Dad strides toward it, with a "DD" design on his shirt and a huge wrench in his hand. |
| Mom helps with your homework. | You and Mom are at a table covered with school papers. You have a lightbulb growing out of your head, and Mom is reaching over to turn on the switch. |

········

# MOMS AND DADS NEED LAUGHS, TOO

## *continued*

**3.** Once you have four or five good visual ideas, think them over carefully to see whether they need any words at all. Some may not, but maybe others would be helped by words that also exaggerate, such as "The Car Just Sits There, With *Daring Dad* Its Only Hope!"

**4.** If you decide to use words to help build each drawing, experiment with weird, cartoonish ways to letter them, right on your scrap-paper drawings. That will give you an idea about how everything will fit together in the final version.

**5.** Then pile up all your scrap paper, to think about what the right order would be for the drawings. To make your card work as a strip, having a story line or a time order might help.

But unless you want to have each drawing lead logically to the next, don't worry too much about how the strip is organized. Maybe your original headline idea will be good enough to make the drawings work as a series.

**6.** Now comes the part that will take some time. Get your clean paper and the colored markers, and use the rough, scrap-paper sketches as models for your finished drawings. Make them as detailed as you can, so that each shows your mother or father that you pay close attention to what goes on every day. That's what will get the laughs.

There's only one risk in doing a comic-strip card. Everybody could like it so much that it will become a tradition, with every holiday needing its own strip. But think about it: Would that be so bad?

### WORD WIZARDRY

### TRADITIONAL COMIC-STRIP WORDS:

Amazing!
Astounding!
Bizarre!
Death-defying!
Unbelievable!

. . . . . . . .
# ACTUALLY, EVERYBODY NEEDS LAUGHS
. . . . . . . . . . . . . . . . . . . .

**T**hink about your favorite newspaper comic strip for a minute. What's funny about it: the main characters, the weird problems they have, the stories that unfold, or simply the fact that something unpredictable happens every day?

If you check out the strip for a week and take time to analyze what makes it work, you may be surprised by how much you discover. It could be enough to get you started on designing your own strip.

### Here's what you need:

*A week's worth of the daily comic pages*
*Scissors and tape*
*15 sheets of paper, all clean*
*A set of colored pencils*

### Here's what you do:

1. Cut out all seven days of your favorite strip. Tape each to a sheet of paper, across the top. Then spread the sheets out on a desk or table, to start looking for what's the same every day.

   - Does the strip always appear as either three or four panels?

   - Is there only one joke per strip, always located in the last panel? Or are there several laughs per strip, scattered around?

   - Do the laughs depend mainly on something the characters *do,* or on what they *say*?

   - Is the main character always there in the strip, or missing sometimes?

2. Answers to those questions will give you an idea of how the surface features of the strip are designed, but they won't do much with the most important question.

   The answer to why the strip is funny almost always lies much deeper, down so far in its design that you'll have to consider some harder questions.

   - Who does the main character seem to represent? Do you "see yourself" when you follow the strip across all seven sheets? Do you think most other readers would also see themselves, or is the character too specialized for that?

   - What typical story line do you see on the sheets? Do the characters always run into frustrations and defeats, or do they occasionally win out? Is the world of the strip set up to work against them? Or are they their own worst enemies? A little of both?

· · · · · · · ·
# ACTUALLY, EVERYBODY NEEDS LAUGHS
## *continued*

- Are you supposed to laugh with them or at them? What keeps you coming back to the strip every day?

Spend enough time with the seven sheets to consider each one of those questions seriously, because they'll take you deeper into the sources of the strip's laughs.

3. Then get out the eighth sheet of paper, and make quick notes about your reactions to all the questions above. Don't try to be too neat or detailed; just get your ideas down fast.

4. Keep those notes handy while you look back at the seven daily strips. Then pick out one strip and use the space below it to sketch out a *different* version of it.

   - Try subtracting one of the characters or adding one to see what could happen to the joke.

   - See if changing some of the details in one or two panels would make the joke better.

   - Try starting with the last panel, to see whether a potential new joke could be developed.

Quickly sketch whatever occurs to you, so that your own version appears right below the taped-on strip.

5. As soon as you feel you're running out of new ideas, look back at your notes and pick out another strip. This time, concentrate just on the words used.

   - Can you change the story simply by changing what the characters say?

   - Could there be *two* jokes in the strip, both based on the same key word?

   - What if two characters completely misunderstand a key word?

Do all the same art and writing work with at least two more of the strips, so that you try out as many new ideas as possible.

6. Then look back at what you've done. Compare your own ideas with the published ones, and think about how good yours could be after additional work.

## ACTUALLY, EVERYBODY NEEDS LAUGHS

### *continued*

What you may find are the beginnings of a whole new comic-strip idea, so different from the original that you'll want to keep developing it. Once you know how to move ideas around and how to keep searching for laughs, maybe you'll want to do more as a cartoonist.

It's certainly possible, because you do have seven clean sheets of paper still in front of you. Try filling them up.

#### WORD WIZARDRY

Ask a librarian where to find these classic comic strips. The art might give you some ideas.
*Felix the Cat*
*The Yellow Kid*
*Asterix*
*Plastic Man*

........

# UPGRADE YOUR HOME PAGE
## TO *WWW.YUKYUKYUK*

. . . . . . . . . . . . . . . . . . .

**I**f you already have a home page, or you've seen how to build one on page 183, you may want to consider improving it by adding some laughs. The Internet is already full of sites with jokes, comic strips, and cartoons, but people are always looking for new and better material.

The problem is that a monitor screen isn't exactly the best place to make laughs happen. It's flat, not much bigger than a piece of paper, and difficult and expensive to fill in with art. But the good part is that screens are ideal for short jokes laid out only in words. The blank space around the joke makes the reader concentrate on it.

You can also change jokes every day if you want, or ask people to e-mail you the best ones they know. Maybe your page could become the electronic home for your Comedy Club.

### Here's what you need:

*Pencil and paper*
*A home page you can use*

### Here's what you do:

**1.** Think about the kinds of short, tight jokes that look good on the small area of a screen.

For a start, here are some types to consider:

- Question-and-answer jokes
- Joking versions of movie, book, or song titles
- Joking versions of statements made by politicians or athletes

········

# UPGRADE YOUR HOME PAGE
## TO *WWW.YUKYUKYUK*

*continued*

2. Recognize that creating new laughs within formats so well known isn't particularly easy. So many jokes already exist that you'll have to work at it for a bit. But once you get rolling, you'll probably find that the second, third, fourth, and even twentieth jokes will come to you much faster than the first one you try.

3. So pick up the pencil, go to the paper, and see what you can do to come up with ten short jokes. To start, you might want to try working on one of the oldest jokes around.

   - Question: Why did the chicken cross the road?
   - Answer:

     _____.

   What can you possibly say that's new? Think about it. Do any of these give you ideas for playing with the chicken question?

   - Answer: He got tired of waiting for the road to cross him.
   - Answer: The other chickens egged him on.
   - Answer: Chickens read backwards, so he thought "Stop" meant "Pots."

   - Answer: He was being paid by the step, not the hour.

4. If you don't like question-and-answer jokes, think about titles. Maybe you can make a "Top Ten Movies to Avoid" list. Try out ridiculous titles, such as *Lethal Armageddon Secret Impact Force XIII*.

   Don't forget books. *Mister Curious Tours the World of Placemats* could be another candidate for a Top Ten list.

5. Keep going until you have a supply you really like. Then decide whether you want to put them all on your home page together or space them out, so that there's one a day or one a week.

   What you do next will depend on how your home page works, so make sure that you can see how to get the jokes worked in as changes or additions. Be careful, too, when you type in the words; misspellings or incorrect punctuation can ruin written jokes.

### WORD WIZARDRY

Why is it "the Net?" Do people shoot basketballs at it, or go fishing with it?

# 3. BECOME A POET AND STORYTELLER

*I*magine people wanting to read your every word. They want you to write stories. They want you to create poems. They want to hear from you.

How do you go about becoming a creative writer of that sort?

You begin by making up your own rules. A poem or story is all yours, not anybody else's. You don't have to write poems with the same rhymes and rhythms that you may have seen in other poems. You can dream up your own favorite rhythms and patterns. You don't have to use rhymes at all.

IMAGINATION

You may read poems that use elaborate language from long ago. Old ways of writing are certainly fun to figure out. You can get interested in talking about "thou" and "thine" instead of "you" and "yours." But you don't have to write in any special language yourself. You can write in the words you use every day. Your poems and stories can be as simple or as complex as you want

You can choose your own subjects, too. Many poems are about love and the meaning of life and religion. You can write about those important subjects, or you can write about anything else. You can write about baseball or homework or your parents—or, maybe best of all, yourself.

You can use your own poems and stories to explain things to yourself, to solve your problems, and to grow and develop within yourself.

How do you get started on a poem or story? You may need to exercise. You can exercise your imagination in just the way you might practice free throws or guitar. If you exercise enough, you could end up with a truly wild and wonderful imagination.

. . . . . . . .
# EXERCISE YOUR COLORFUL IMAGINATION

. . . . . . . . . . . . . . . . . . . . .

**W**hen people think about colors, often they make connections with feelings or thoughts. The color may represent something grand and abstract, good or bad, lucky or unlucky.

But colors do not mean the same around the world. In North America, we may think of red on a sign as a bright warning of danger or trouble, a time to be careful. In Asia, though, you might decorate a New Year's or wedding celebration all in red because that would mean joy and good wishes. On a flag, red may stand for great ideas, such as liberty and courage. But then, too, you might see red as the symbol of anger or the blood of war.

You may think of black and white as opposite colors. But they can have the same meanings. For example, if you were drawing a picture of a devil or a fearful demon—or of a very sad person dressed in mourning attire—would you color black clothes? Black can stand for sorrow and death, maybe because it is the color of night and people often fear darkness.

But white can also stand for sorrow and death. Would you color a ghost white? Some people imagine white as the color of fear and death because white is the color of bones. It all depends on the connections you make.

Here's one way to exercise your imagination and perhaps think up a few ideas for your poems and stories. Just think about colors, only think of them so that you twist and turn your point of view.

1. You'll notice that the sky is never just plain dull blue. Look at the sky, and decide the exact colors it is right now. Since you're exercising your imagination, feel free to make up a color or combination of colors. (Use your imagination, and perhaps you can sense the stars still shining even when you cannot see them during the daytime.)

2. Use your imagination to make connections between a color and a sound. You're not making a real-world connection; you're making a connection of imagination. For example, what color is the sound of an oboe? What color is the sound of bees buzzing? What colors are the sounds of people laughing, scolding, shouting, or whining?

3. Think from the point of view of a bee. A bee can see colors beyond the range of a human eye. A bee can see colors at each end of the color spectrum, infrared and ultraviolet. You cannot see those colors. How do they look in your imagination?

# EXERCISE YOUR COLORFUL IMAGINATION
## *continued*

I think that I shall never see a poem lovely as a bee!

INK

4. Think from the point of view of a hurricane, a volcano, or a huge killer wave. What colors and patterns do you imagine?
5. Try writing a poem about the colors you imagine. You can write about a different color in each line, or you can write a poem all about the different ways one color can feel to you.

### WORD WIZARDRY

You're using your imagination to make out-of-the-ordinary connections between things that are not usually connected. The human eye can distinguish more than seven million shades of color. Plus we can imagine even more. That's a colorful imagination.

· · · · · · · ·
# EXERCISE AN ANIMAL IMAGINATION
· · · · · · · · · · · · · · · · · · ·

Imagine you can see from the point of view of an animal, any animal you like. Animal thoughts are good exercise for your imagination. Practice on a few ideas. You may want to write a poem or story about your strange animal thoughts:

1. Perhaps the animal you choose knows no human words. How could you think if you did not think in words? Remember, you could probably still communicate well with other animals, maybe even in complicated ways.

2. Or maybe the animal you imagine knows just a few human words. Your pet dog probably knows quite a few words. Chimpanzees, gorillas, and dolphins can learn human words, too. Your cat may know what "Here, kitty, kitty" means. But human beings had to teach them human words. And who knows? The animal you imagine may have a rare and strange connection with human words, something the human beings don't realize.

3. Imagine thinking by smell. An animal may have a strong sense of smell far beyond human ability. So if you think from the point of view of an animal, you may need to think in smells.

4. An animal's eyes may see differently from a human's, too. Imagine seeing hundreds of images all at once the way a fly does. Or imagine seeing as far across the world as a giraffe can, with its long neck and long-distance vision.

5. Exercise your imagination on animals, and picture yourself driven by instincts that work inside you and control your actions and thoughts. Suppose you are a monarch butterfly beginning the long migration from Canada to Mexico, or a bird flying from South America to the Arctic twice a year, right on the exact schedule nature has already determined. Suppose you think like a leopard finding a good antelope to hunt—an antelope with an inborn set of instincts to watch out for the leopard.

6. You may even want to exercise your imagination on the thoughts of an animal that doesn't seem very smart to humans (although the animal may think to itself that it's smart). What if you were a dinosaur with a gigantic body and a tiny brain in your head? Your tiny brainpower might not reach as far as your tail, so farther down your body you could need a separate set of nerves, a sort of second

. . . . . . . .
# EXERCISE AN ANIMAL IMAGINATION
## *continued*

tiny brain, just to manage your tail. Exercise your imagination on that tail kind of thinking.

7. Exercise your imagination on all the other ways animals are different from humans. What if you were a thoroughbred racing horse? You'd have your own horse ideas about racing and winning.

### WORD WIZARDRY

Here's another way to stretch your animal imagination. Think of animals in groups, and think up the just right name for the groups. A large number of ducks, for example, is not just a group of ducks—it's a paddling of ducks.

· · · · · · · ·

# EXERCISE AN ANIMAL IMAGINATION
## *continued*

You can exercise your imagination by naming even more animal groups to fit in with these:

| | |
|---|---|
| a crash of rhinoceroses | a gaggle of geese |
| a leap of leopards | a parliament of birds |
| a plague of locusts | a pride of lions |
| a school of fishes | a skulk of foxes |

Now think of a few human groups. What do you call a gathering of fourth-graders? What do you call a group of annoying little brothers or a group of mothers watching a soccer game? What do you call a group of all the people you like or dislike the most?

## EXERCISE YOUR SECRET IMAGINATION

If you exercise your imagination, you may find that suddenly you have the ability to think and feel and imagine many ways at once. You have secret depths to your mind. A good imagination is complicated business—and lots of fun.

Here are ways to exercise your imagination on opposites and secrets. You may want to write a poem or story about how many ways you can imagine opposites.

1. Suppose you know something is supposed to be beautiful, but secretly you think it's ugly—or the other way around. Think of a worm, mold on cheese, or fungus on tree bark. Can you imagine any of those in a way that makes them look good to you? Could a flower look ugly?
2. Remember some really bad weather. Did you actually like something about the snow or wind or rain?
3. Suppose you can find something to admire about a person whom no one else likes. Or maybe you secretly don't quite like the most popular kid in school.

· · · · · · · ·

# EXERCISE YOUR SECRET IMAGINATION

## *continued*

4.  Suppose you hate something, such as homework or a particular food, that is supposed to be good for you. You may even agree that doing homework without music or television makes for better homework. You may admit that if you go to bed early, you are more wide awake in the morning. But can you see the opposite point of view?

5.  Suppose you have to say you're sorry for something you said or did—but you don't really feel sorry.

6.  Suppose you have changed your mind about something, so you believe the opposite of what you thought before. As you grow up, you may see opposites and complications all around you. If you can think in opposites, you can think like a creative poet or story writer. As the poet David McCord said, it's all like hot coffee dripping from an icicle.

### WORD WIZARDRY

If you like to draw, find a good proverb and draw a picture of it. A picture is always a good way to exercise your imagination. Try one of these as a proverb picture:

- We're all in the same boat.
- No pain, no gain.
- Finders keepers, losers weepers.
- A leopard can't change its spots.
- The pen is mightier than the sword.
- Hitch your wagon to a star.

# CONDUCT A SIMILE SURVEY

**A** good writer thinks of odd comparisons and contradictions. But so does everyone else. Conduct a survey, and find out.

For your survey, ask people ten ways to say that someone is very smart or very annoying. Ask five ways to say a dog is badly behaved. Ask a few ways to say that it's a nice day.

You'll find that people immediately begin to talk in similes and metaphors.

What are similes and metaphors? In a simile, you compare one thing to another by using the words *like* or *as*.

> That dog acts like King Kong.
> That dog behaves like a bull in a china shop.

In a metaphor, you compare things directly, as if you imagine one thing exactly like another.

> So you think you're Mr. Einstein.
> That girl is a ray of sunshine.

You may hear a few weird and funny comparisons.

> That dog is so crazy he must have a geranium in his cranium.
> She's not the brightest bulb on the Christmas tree.

· · · · · · · ·
# CONDUCT A SIMILE SURVEY
## *continued*

If you don't want to do a survey, then just listen to people talk. You'll hear plenty of similes and metaphors.

Here's a way to exercise your imagination on your similes and metaphors. Make your comparisons really weird. You'll like them better that way.

- As green as . . .
- As tall as . . .
- As noisy as . . .
- As gloomy as . . .
- As happy as . . .
- The traffic is as . . . as . . .
- The fourth-graders are like . . .
- The weather is like . . .

### WORD WIZARDRY

You may want to draw a picture of a funny simile or metaphor. To get started, try one of these:

- You go bananas.
- You're in a jam.
- You carry the weight of the world on your shoulders.
- You have a green thumb.
- You see the world through rose-colored glasses.
- You bite the hand that feeds you.
- You chase up a blind alley.

. . . . . . . .
# GET RIGHT INTO WRITING A POEM
. . . . . . . . . . . . . . . . . . . . .

**T**o write a poem, you'll want to invent and imagine the most wonderful things, with a display of words that truly sound right. Your poem can be as strange as you want. You can make it different from anyone else's poem.

First, choose a subject. It can be any subject, but you ought to feel strongly about it. Here are a few ideas for subjects, just to get you started:

1.  Write a poem about something that is different in your life. Perhaps the difference in your life is that you're growing up and feeling your body and your mind change as you get older. Perhaps your family or your friendships are changing.
2.  Write a poem about something that strikes you as really funny or really sad. Think about how you actually do feel, not how you think you're supposed to feel.
3.  Write a poem about something you wish. Imagine what would happen if you got exactly what you wish. While you're thinking about your wish, remember the proverb that you should be careful what you wish—if your wishes came true, you might end up surprised, disappointed, or even scared.

. . . . . . . .

# GET RIGHT INTO WRITING A POEM
### *continued*

4. Write a poem from a peculiar point of view. Imagine discovering a secret that no one else knows. Perhaps you suddenly understand what it feels like to be a mosquito, a dinosaur, a computer, a planet, or a snowstorm.
5. Write a poem of comparisons. Compare opposites, such as something very big and something very little, or something that has feelings and something that does not have feelings.
6. Write a poem about your favorite music.

Find a subject that's exciting, and then just start writing. You can always worry about the details later. First, get your feelings on paper. Then go on to think of the design for your poem.

### WORD WIZARDRY

One way to get started on a poem is to begin with the first line of another poem. Then write your own lines that follow. Try a funny twist on a popular song or a nursery rhyme:

> There was an old woman who lived in a shoe.
> Star light, star bright . . .

Or write your own poem starting with one line from a serious poem. The poet Walt Whitman began part of a poem this way:

> I think I could turn, and live with animals.

You can exercise your own imagination on why you might enjoy living with animals instead of people.

# PUT TOGETHER A CREATIVE TOOL KIT

**A**ll poems and stories have some sort of design. A creative writer plans ahead. You can put together your own creative tool kit so that you can play with design whenever you wish.

Here's what you need for your creative tool kit:

1. Maybe you'll want your poem to have symmetry and repetition. That's a balance where one part closely resembles another part. (Look at a butterfly or a leaf—or even your own body. If you drew a line right down the middle, you'd find that each half was almost exactly like the other half.) Maybe you'll want your poem to repeat a first word or phrase in each line. Maybe you'll want to write your poem in a certain number of lines, with one line repeating in a pattern. You'll see a pattern like that in the lyrics of almost all songs and ballads.

2. Maybe you'll decide on a rhythm for your poem, perhaps something like the rhythm of a drumbeat.

3. You may want your poem to rhyme. You're probably used to seeing rhymes in poems and songs. If you're interested in rhyme, try keeping a journal of words that rhyme. You may like your rhymes to be funny, like the end of one of David McCord's verses:

> Tired of this rhyme?
> I'm.

········
# PUT TOGETHER A CREATIVE TOOL KIT
## *continued*

4.  You may want alliteration for one of your creative tools. That's a repetition of sounds, usually in titles or in the first sounds of words in a poem. You can see alliteration go to extremes in tongue twisters:

    She sells seashells down by the sea shore.
    For fabulous fine fresh fat finny fish, phone Fred.

5.  Finish your poem by making sure the grammar, spelling, and punctuation are all in order. But save that step for the end. Think of everything else first.

### WORD WIZARDRY

Do you know the favorite rhythm for poems in the English language? It's iambic pentameter. That's a beat of one weak syllable followed by one strong syllable. If you were playing a drum, that might sound like ba BOOM, ba BOOM. Then repeat it five times, and you have one good line of iambic pentameter. As you might guess, the root word, penta-, means five. Here's an example from the poet John Keats:

Bright star! Would I were steadfast as thou art.

Divide it by five like this:
1. Bright star!
2. Would I
3. Were stead-
4. Fast as
5. Thou art.

· · · · · · · ·
# WRITE A BOWWOW POEM
· · · · · · · · · · · · · · · · · · · ·

**S**ometimes poets and storytellers use words that sound exactly like what they mean. *Bowwow* sounds a bit like a dog barking. *Meow* sounds somewhat like a cat. Think also of words like *tinkle* or *sparkle, dingdong, hallelujah, chickadee,* or *buzz.*

Or think of the verse about the mouse running up the clock. Doesn't *hickory dickory dock* sound like a clock striking? It's an attempt to capture a sound in words.

The long name for this sort of word that sounds like what it means is *onomatopoeia.* You may want to make a list of the onomatopoeic words you come across. If you especially like some of them, list them in your creative person's tool kit.

Here's an example from Edgar Allan Poe's poem "The Bells," written to sound just like bells. Even if you don't know right now what the words *runic* or *tintinnabulation* mean, you can tell that the poem sounds just like bells, perhaps bells from a church or a monument:

> Keeping time, time, time,
> In a sort of Runic rhyme,
> To the tintinnabulation that so musically wells
> From the bells, bells, bells, bells.

Poe repeats words so that they sound almost like the repeating sounds of the bells, bells, bells.

POETRY CAN BE VERY MOOOO-VING

# WRITE A BOWWOW POEM
### *continued*

See if you can write a poem that uses an onomatopoeic word in every line. You may want to try a poem about animals barking, meowing, warbling, clucking, oinking, hissing, and neighing. Or you may want to try a poem about people who giggle, grumble, gargle, gurgle, snort, snore, whine, whimper, and whisper.

## WORD WIZARDRY

You can guess that the word *tintinnabulation* means "the ringing of bells." *Runic* refers to an ancient Scandinavian way of writing, from so long ago that hardly anyone knows what the writing means any longer. So the word has come to mean something mysterious and magical, repeating in strange patterns over and over—just like bells.

· · · · · · · ·
# Write Two Poems for Someone Special
· · · · · · · · · · · · · · · · · · · ·

**H**ere are two funny ways to write a poem. Maybe you know someone special who would like one.

1.  Write a poem so that the first letter of each line spells a name. For example, write a poem of six lines for your mother. The first word of the first line begins with "M." The second line begins with "O." In the next four lines, you go right on through "T – H – E – R."

2.  Write a picture poem. That's a poem that has a shape to it that matches the subject. Write a Valentine's Day poem that is in the shape of a heart. Write a poem about an alligator that is in the shape of a long alligator tail. Write a welcome-home poem that is in the shape of a house. This sort of poem is especially fun to write on a computer or typewriter.

## Word Wizardry

Some little poems even carry scientific messages. If you can't remember the difference between the stalagmites and the stalactites in caves, try this.

The mites go up
And the tites come down.

· · · · · · · ·
# WRITE HAIKU
· · · · · · · · · · · · · · · · · · · ·

**J**apanese haiku (pronounced HIGH-koo) are different from other poems. They are short, containing only three lines. When you write haiku, you leave out rhymes. You leave out any beat or rhythm. You don't repeat words much. You don't need to write in whole sentences.

Instead, you think of an image of nature. Think about how you are connected to nature. Think about leaves and flowers, trees and rivers, birds and butterflies. Concentrate until a single, simple picture comes into your mind. Then work on describing just that one image. Write in the present, as if you were just seeing this image, and make every word count. Here is the pattern to follow:

1.  Write the first line with five syllables.
2.  Write the second line with seven syllables.
3.  Write the third line with five syllables again.

You may find that writing a simple poem can be more complicated than you think.

. . . . . . . .
# WRITE HAIKU
### *continued*

## WORD WIZARDRY

Which is the better idea for a poem? A boy plucks the wings from a dragonfly. Without wings, the bright red body of the dragonfly looks like a red pepper pod. Or turn the story around. A boy sees a bright red pepper pod. He imagines it with wings, and suddenly he pictures a dragonfly taking off into the noon sun. Now he imagines life and movement, instead of destruction and stillness.

The Japanese poet Basho, who lived more than 300 years ago, told this story. Here is one haiku image Basho created. See if you can imagine what Basho saw:

> First dawn: Young white fish
> Shining in emerald white
> Hardly an inch long.

# WRITE EVEN MORE JAPANESE POETRY

**H**aiku are always about an image of nature or a season. For a change, try writing *senryu*. That's another type of poem from Japan. This type (named for the poet who invented it) is just like haiku, with the same number of lines and syllables, but you write about any subject you please. You don't need to be serious, either. You can write a funny poem if you want.

### WORD WIZARDRY

You can write poems on any subject, even subjects you learn in school. Carl Sandburg once wrote a funny poem called "Arithmetic." When you try to remember the multiplication tables, remember this line from that poem:

> Arithmetic is where you have to multiply—
> and you carry the multiplication table in
> your head and hope you won't lose it.

David McCord wrote poems that list the hardest spelling words. Here's how his poem "Spelling Bee" begins:

> It takes a good speller
> to spell cellar.

........
# GET RIGHT INTO WRITING A STORY
.........................

**I**f you like looking around for ideas for stories, you'll see some **every day.** Perhaps you **notice** a problem between two people at school. **That could** be the beginning of the plot for a story. Perhaps you meet **an interesting** person and you imagine a character for a story. Or maybe **you imagine** the setting first, what it would be like to live in a jungle, **a desert, or an** ancient castle.

Once you imagine plot, character, or setting, you're on **your way to** developing a story.

Have you noticed that stories have a form to them? Although it may not be so obvious, a story has a form in the same way that a joke, a limerick, or a poem has a form.

### Here's how to begin:

1. Think of a general idea for your story. Your idea can be something directly from your own life, or, if you want, your idea can be something strange and exotic from your imagination.
   - What would it be like to be locked inside school overnight?
   - How do you handle teasing and threats from a bully?

- How would people behave on a ship hurtling through space?
- What if an animal chose not to behave the way people expect?

2. Limit your story somewhat. A short story has space to deal with only a few characters—and usually with only one major action, problem, or conflict.

3. Write down a simple introduction. If you don't think of the perfect opening right away, then just write something plain and direct:

   This is a story about . . .

4. Decide on a point of view. You may want to tell your story through an "I" character (first person), as if that person were the one telling the story. The "I" character can be a lot like you or not at all like you. But if you tell the story through an "I"

**69**
•

. . . . . . . .

# GET RIGHT INTO WRITING A STORY

## *continued*

character, you tell only the observations and thoughts of that person. Or you may want to tell your story in the third person ("he," "she," "they," "it") so that you can reveal the viewpoint and thoughts of any character, even an animal.

- I pounded on the door. I couldn't believe I was locked in that dreadful dark basement. Surely there must be some way out. Surely someone would hear me soon.

- Max the Bully was dreaded throughout the neighborhood.

- She looked out the porthole at the darkness of the space outside. For the first time, she was not entirely happy to be on her way to the moons of Jupiter.

- I am the most powerful bull in Spain. But I refuse to fight in the ring. The bullfighters can wave all the red flags they want. I won't fight.

5. Decide on one major action or conflict. Perhaps it is something that happens to your main character. Perhaps it is something your character decides as a way of solving a problem. If you don't think of just the right words at first, just write something simple: "This is what happened . . ."

- In the dark basement of the school, I would just have to find something to do until morning—preferably something that would keep me from being scared.

- Max the Bully found himself surrounded by angry people. They all seemed to have a lot to say to him.

- She calculated that on that particular day, only one of Jupiter's moons would allow for a safe landing. Unfortunately, her partner did not agree.

- I could see the pasture in the distance. If only I could get there, I would be safe, far away from the bullfighting ring.

6. Bring the conflict or problem of the story to a resolution. Your resolution can be happy or sad, funny or surprising, weird or just what the reader might expect. But it must give a sense of conclusion. If you wish, you can always write a simple conclusion: "This is how it turned out . . ."

- I really had a fine time in the basement overnight. But I'll never go anywhere again without checking the locks.

- Max the Bully was really a good guy at heart.

. . . . . . . .
# GET RIGHT INTO WRITING A STORY
## *continued*

- She braced herself against the wind, and stepped onto the hot, sulfuric sand of the best of Jupiter's moons. She was the first after all.

- I munched some clover. Maybe I'd try some corn later. There was plenty for everybody— and no bullfighter in sight.

7. You may wish to add one more element to your story, a surprise. Or if you wish, you may want to add a last comment: "This is what I thought about it afterward."

  - I decided never to tell anyone about my night in the basement. After all, I'm a role model. I'm the principal of the school.

- **After he finished the training course and got some proper attention from people, Max the Bully turned out to be the best behaved dog in the neighborhood.**

- **People seem to have an inborn desire** to travel, to explore, to learn, not to be stopped, no matter what the dangers. She knew she would lose her life there on the burning surface of Jupiter's moon, but she decided this journey was worth all of that, worth any sacrifice.

- Now I have proved that I am truly the most powerful bull in Spain. I decided the course of my own life.

Now you have the basic form for your story. Think it over, and rewrite the story so that you have the best possible words. Then go over it one last time to make sure the grammar, spelling, and punctuation are all in good order.

### WORD WIZARDRY

You can have fun writing poems, plays, or stories with your friends or classmates. Each person gets to add ideas, characters, and phrases. Or each person gets to act out a character, as if you had your own theater. Just be sure to let each person have an equal chance to contribute. Several years ago, someone with a good imagination started a very strange book. The idea was that this book would travel all across the United States, from one town to another. People would come to see the book and each person would pick up

# GET RIGHT INTO WRITING A STORY
## *continued*

a big pen and add just one sentence to the story. The story would twist and turn, and eventually become very long. So far, more than 6,000 writers have put in one sentence each. (Maybe the book will come to your hometown and you'll have a chance to write in it.) The hope is that someday this unusual book will rest in a museum, where everyone can read it. This is how it starts:

> Once upon a time, high up north on the top of a mountain, Ben was pondering. Will it ever end?

# WRITE POEMS AND STORIES THE GOOD OLD-FASHIONED WAY

Write a poem or a story about a problem you have and how you might go about solving it. Great kings and queens, governors, and soldiers from long ago wrote poems as a way to think over their problems and make some of their wisest decisions.

If you write a story about a problem, you can try various solutions and imagine what would happen before you try it in real life. You're exercising your imagination in the best possible way.

# 4. Design Your Own Fancy Lettering, Cards, Signs, and Books

*U*sually, you buy what you need for special occasions: cards, stationery, envelopes, signs, and books. It's just a trip to the store. But how would you like to make your own special creations? No store will have anything like them.

Would you also like to look deep into handwriting? Maybe you'd like to find out something about other people's personalities just by looking at their handwriting. Would you like to practice your own elegant and artistic penmanship? Would you like to design a signature you can be proud of all your life?

Here's how.

## DESIGN YOUR OWN SIGNATURE

**W**hat are the words you will write most often during the course of your life? The answer is the words of your own name.

You'll want your signature to show something about what sort of person you are. You'll want it somehow special, unique, and important. You'll probably be using your signature every day all your life. It's worth putting in some practice on it.

### Here's how to design your signature:

1. Decide how you will sign your name. Perhaps you want your full name as your signature. People do that sometimes because they don't want to be confused with another person. If your name is George Washington, for instance, you might want to sign as George Stephen Washington. Or if your father or mother has the same name as you, you might want to make sure your name stands out: Anton Cruz, Jr.

Sometimes people decide to add some distinction to a common name: Jane Alicia Maria Gardiner Doe. Or sometimes people just like to sign fancy names all in a row: John Jacob Jingleheimer Smith. Perhaps you want to write your name with an initial in the middle: Ashley A. Allen. Or maybe you just want to keep your name plain and simple: José Alvarez.

2. Decide how fancy or plain you want your signature to be. In school, you often practice handwriting that is neat and

## · · · · · · · ·
# DESIGN YOUR OWN SIGNATURE
## *continued*

easy to read. But sometimes, away from school, people decide on just the opposite, a signature that is hard to read. Maybe they want a signature that shows how creative or interesting they are. Or maybe they want a signature that is difficult to imitate.

3. Now decide what characteristics you want to show in your signature. Many people believe they can look at handwriting and analyze personality. Maybe they can tell a lot about you just from your signature—and maybe they can't. But when you are just forming your own special style of handwriting, think about what characteristics make you look like a strong, smart person.

### WORD WIZARDRY

Sometime when you're in a museum or historic building, look at the signatures of famous people. Often you'll find that you can hardly read the names. The signatures may be elaborate and important-looking—and very difficult to forge. You'll notice that legal documents often ask you to sign your name and then also print it neatly. Lawyers are used to a lot of hard-to-read signatures.

# ANALYZE HANDWRITING

**I**f you know how to analyze handwriting, you could help catch a criminal by studying a check to see if the signature is genuine or fake. You could work for a company and study the job applications to see what handwriting shows about people.

Handwriting analysis can go only so far, though. Just from looking at handwriting, you cannot tell the difference between a criminal and an honest person.

But you can have fun with handwriting analysis. Maybe you can use it to figure out just a few secrets about personality.

***Here's what you may see when you match handwriting and personality:***

1. Look at how you cross your *t*'s:

   - Crossed very high—You may be intelligent, ambitious, and creative.

   - Crossed in the center—You may have a well-balanced personality.

   - Crossed very low—You may be kind, humble, and unassuming.

   - Crossed with an upward slant—You may be optimistic and cheerful.

   - Crossed more to the right—You may be an enthusiastic and active person.

   - Not crossed at all—Were you careless when you wrote that or in too much of a hurry?

2. Look at how you loop letters like *h* and *l*, *p* and *g* or *q*.

   - Long, wide loops—You may be energetic and vigorous. You probably like sports.

   - High, open loops—Are you intelligent, ambitious, and idealistic?

   - Narrow loops—Are you a careful and cautious person?

   - Tall, closed loops—You may be self-confident. Do you like to be the leader of a group?

3. Look at how you dot your *i*'s:

   - Dotted with a circle—Are you showing that you're artistic? Do you want to be different from other people?

   - Not dotted at all—Are you often careless and hurried?

· · · · · · · ·

# ANALYZE HANDWRITING

## *continued*

**4.** Look at how large your writing is and how it slants:

- Very small writing—Perhaps you are precise and careful in whatever you do.
- Very large writing—Do you want to stand out from others? Are you extravagant with money?
- Very little slant, straight-up letters—You may be intelligent, independent, and self-reliant.
- Upward slant—Perhaps you are cheerful and optimistic.
- Disconnected letters—Are you impractical but also creative and imaginative?
- Many extra small lines in the letters—You may be quick to anger.

### WORD WIZARDRY

The science of analyzing handwriting is called *graphology.* You can see the source word, *graph,* in other words about writing and drawing, such as *graphics* or *calligraphy.* You can see the root *-ology* in other words about study, such as *biology.*

# PRACTICE THE ART OF BEAUTIFUL HANDWRITING

Calligraphy is the art of beautiful writing, and a good way to create an award, holiday cards, or fancy invitations. Calligraphy creations make good gifts. You can use your fine handwriting to copy and decorate a bookmark or bookplate, or a favorite poem or proverb for someone special.

### Here's what you need:

*Calligraphy pens or fine-pointed markers (there are also pens specially made for left-handed writers)*

*Bottled ink, if you decide to use calligraphy pens*

*Graph or lined paper*

*A ruler, a pencil, and an eraser*

### Here's how to practice beautiful handwriting:

1. If you are using calligraphy pens for the first time, practice filling them with ink. Then practice writing anything at all, until you get used to the way the pens work.

2. As you practice, try drawing the thickest line your pen or marker can make. That's the "pen width."

3. Choose a line on your paper where your letters will sit. That's the baseline. Then use a pencil to mark other lines you'll need:

   • Mark a line above the baseline for the top of the letters that don't go up and down, such as the lowercase letter *x*. That's the x-line. It ought to be one or two graph squares or four pen widths high.

   • Mark a line above the x-line for tall letters like *d, h,* or *t* to reach. That's the ascender line. It should be one or two graph squares or two pen widths higher than the top of the x-line.

   • Mark a line under the baseline for long letters like *p, g,* and *q* to reach. That's the descender line. It should be one or two graph squares or two pen widths lower than the baseline.

········

# PRACTICE THE ART OF BEAUTIFUL HANDWRITING

## *continued*

- Mark the line for uppercase letters to reach. It should be two or four graph squares or six pen widths above the baseline.

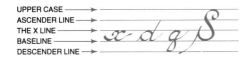

UPPER CASE ——→
ASCENDER LINE ——→
THE X LINE ——→
BASELINE ——→
DESCENDER LINE ——→

4. Practice writing on the lines you marked. Before you draw letters, practice drawing straight lines, both up and down and across.

Then practice drawing straight lines at a slight angle. Try drawing slanted tops and bottoms on your lines. Soon you'll be ready to practice drawing each letter of the alphabet. You'll be developing your own creative style.

5. Practice dotting your *i*'s with a diamond dot.

6. Practice leaving a small space between each letter, about one pen width.

7. When you're done, let the ink dry for five or ten minutes. Then erase any leftover pencil markings.

When you've practiced enough, try drawing something very special. You deserve an award.

### WORD WIZARDRY

One way to practice fancy writing and drawing is to use two pencils. Tape the pencils together. Then try zigzags, spirals, and ribbons. The effect can be especially good if you use pencils of two different colors.

## BLOCK OUT YOUR OWN PRINTING

$S$uppose you had lived many centuries ago as an important governor, king, or queen. You probably would have worn a large signet ring emblazoned with the initial of your name or your own specially designed seal. Whenever you needed to seal an important document, you could press your ring into soft, warm wax. When the wax cooled and hardened, you'd have a wax impression of your own design.

You can use the same idea (without wax) to print your own fancy letters of the alphabet, initials of a name, and other small designs. You may need adult help with cutting and carving.

### Here's what you need to print this way:

*Scratch paper and a pencil*

*A small mirror, if you wish*

*A cutting board*

*A sharp kitchen or craft knife*

Something to be carved *with the letter or design, such as a potato, a carrot, a rubber eraser, or a block of Styrofoam*

*Paper towels*

Something you can use to print, *such as ink pads, powdered paints, or food-coloring paste with water*

*If you are printing with paint or food coloring, a small disposable container, such as an empty margarine or delicatessen tub*

*If you are printing with paint or food coloring, a small, thin sponge*

Something to print on, *such as paper, poster board, or, if you are using food coloring, a food*

### Here's what you do:

1. Use scratch paper and a pencil to sketch a letter or design. You'll need to draw your letter or design in reverse of the way you want it to look. So you may want to check it with a mirror to make sure you have it right. Rework it until you are happy with the design. Keep it plain and simple.

2. Get out the cutting board and a sharp knife.

   : *Caution: You need adult help*
   : *with cutting.*

3. If you are using a potato, cut it in half. Or cut off the end of a carrot. The goal is to cut a smooth, flat printing surface.

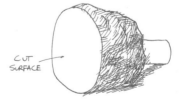

CUT SURFACE

*Hint: If you want, cut the other side of the potato into a handle, so you can keep a good grip as you work with it.*

. . . . . . . .
# BLOCK OUT YOUR OWN PRINTING
## *continued*

4. Next, use a pencil to sketch a letter or design onto the surface of the potato, carrot, rubber eraser, or foam block. Before you begin to cut, you may want to check your letter with the small mirror to be sure it's going to come out the way you want it to.

5. Then use your knife to cut in your design. As you work, use a paper towel to clean off the surface. Cut away from you, and work carefully. Don't cut your design too small, or the pattern won't show well.

   *Caution: You must have adult help with this sort of cutting.*

6. Decide how you want the printing to look. You can use an ink pad to get color, or more than one, so that you can mix different colors. You can also use the disposable container to mix powdered paints, or mix food coloring and water to get an unusual color. When you're done, use the sponge to soak up the paint or food coloring.

7. Then press the design or letter firmly onto the pad or sponge. Try stamping it onto scrap paper to see how it prints. This is your chance to make last-minute changes, if you want.

8. When you are ready for real printing, pencil in some guide-lines on your paper. The lines will help you place your print-ing just where you want it. Then print along the lines. Press your design firmly, and be careful not to smudge.

9. You can print your letter or design over and over for a patterned effect. Or maybe you want to surprise people at lunch. If you're using food coloring, try printing on a food: cookies, toast, sandwiches, or hard-boiled eggs.

### WORD WIZARDRY

Centuries ago, printers had to cut each letter into wood, one at a time. Making books took so long that they were expensive and scarce. Then the famous German printer Johannes Gutenberg invented the first truly movable, reusable type. He'd devised how to use the same metal letters over and over, rearranging them to make pages and then books. He invented the first printing press—or at least the first printing press that actually worked.

........
# MAKE YOUR OWN HOLIDAY CARDS
. . . . . . . . . . . . . . . . . . . .

**Y**ou can make your own one-of-a-kind cards to celebrate a holiday, a birthday, or any other special occasion, with your own custom-made shapes, colors, designs, and printing. This is a good project for a creative person.

### Here's what you need:

*Scrap paper and pencil for practice*

*Card paper, poster board, or another thick paper*

*Scissors*

*Markers or coloring pens, in colors you choose*

*A ruler*

*Household glue or school paste*

### Here are a few tips for making creative holiday cards:

1. Always begin with scrap paper and pencil. A creative person needs to try out new ideas and get in a little practice.

2. When you fold a card, use a ruler or straightedge to get the folds crisp and sharp.

### Here are a few ideas for putting some extra creativity into your cards:

1. As one way to get started, try cutting the paper for your card into a rectangle or square. Then, on another piece of paper, use a pencil to sketch a face and hands (or paws) to peer over the top of the card. When you are happy with your sketch, fill it in with markers or coloring pens. Then cut it out

and paste it so that it appears to be peeking over the top of the card.

2. Cut your card into a long rectangle. Then measure and divide the card into three parts. Fold each end in, toward the middle.

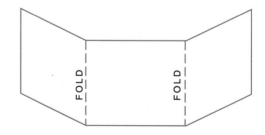

3. If you wish, cut your three-part card into a shape. For example, sketch a kitten or puppy head on the right side and a kitten or puppy tail on the left; the body

· · · · · · · ·

# MAKE YOUR OWN HOLIDAY CARDS

### *continued*

is in the middle. Then cut out the shape of the head, the shape of the tail, and the shape of the body. Now fold the head and tail in toward the center. Color in your card with markers or coloring pens.

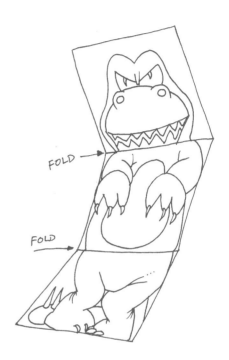

4. Cut your card into a tall, up-and-down rectangle. Then measure and divide the card into three up-and-down parts. Fold the top part and the bottom part in toward the center. Then draw and cut out a design, perhaps a long, tall dinosaur who folds up to be a small creature.

5. Cut strips of construction paper in two colors. Then weave and paste the strips together with contrasting colors.

### WORD WIZARDRY

Think about framing your card. You can cut poster board or cardboard to fit, then write or draw on it, or paste decorations on it.

## ·······
# MAKE A POP-UP CARD
· · · · · · · · · · · · · · · · · · · ·

**H**ere's how to make the best card of all, a pop-up card. Wouldn't your mother, your father, your best friend, or your teacher like to have one for a special occasion?

### Here's what you need:

Scrap paper and pencil

Poster board, card paper, or another thick paper

Scissors

A ruler

Household glue or school paste

Markers or coloring pens, in colors you choose

### Here's how to make a pop-up card:

1. You will probably want to practice on scrap paper first. Just use a pencil to sketch in ideas until you get your pop-up card the way you want it.

2. Fold the paper in half, like this:

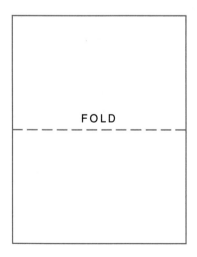

FOLD

3. Use scissors to cut tabs in the paper, like this:

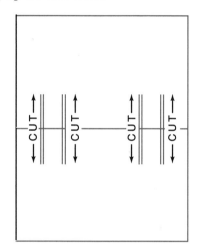

4. Open the folded paper and push the tabs to the inside. Now you have two places to attach your pop-up figures.

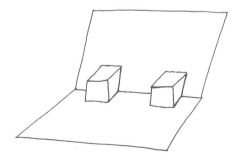

5. On another piece of paper, draw the figures you want

## . . . . . . . .
# MAKE A POP-UP CARD
### *continued*

to pop up. Use a ruler to make sure your figures are the right size to fit inside the card. First, use a pencil to sketch the figures. Then color them with markers or coloring pens. Use scissors to cut out the figures.

6. Use household glue or school paste to attach the figures to the two tabs.

7. If you wish, write a message or greeting on the base beneath your figures. Now try out your pop-up.

### WORD WIZARDRY

People have liked pop-up cards and books ever since they were invented. For more than 200 years now, artists have competed to see who could make the most elaborate and complicated pop-ups. Figures are sometimes controlled by strings or rubber bands. There is even a pop-up paper cheeseburger, with layers of lettuce and tomato that slide into place.

. . . . . . . .
# CREATE ONE-OF-A-KIND STATIONERY WITH ENVELOPES
. . . . . . . . . . . . . . . . . . . .

You can use a computer to design your own stationery, and then copy your design onto fine paper. Whenever you want to write a letter, you'll have unique stationery. Or you can design title headlines for your own newsletter.

You may need someone to help you find all the ways your computer can help.

### Here's how to design stationery on a computer:

1. Decide what sort of information you want to print on each sheet of stationery. You probably want your name and address right at the top, and then perhaps your telephone number or some other information.

2. Choose a font. Most computers offer many styles of type, so you can pick the one that interests you most. You can even choose some that look like handwriting.

3. Choose a point size. Point size measures how large the type will print. For a letterhead or titles, you may want to try 18-point type. Or try 24-point size. Or you can try for a special effect, with your name in a larger point size and your address in smaller type.

*Hint: Look at headlines in a newspaper or chapter titles in a book to see what impression each size makes.*

4. Use the computer to try out different looks for your letterhead. Perhaps you want it in bold type, in italics, or underlined.

5. Key in your words, and think about how you want them to line up. You may want them centered, or at the left margin. You may want a bar or line underneath. Use "preview" to check how your format looks. Then you can change it all around as much as you want. You can try out a variety of fonts, point sizes, and formats until you find which you like best.

6. Now print copies of your stationery, in color if you can. Soon you'll have a pile of fine stationery waiting.

Of course, you can write your

· · · · · · · ·

# CREATE ONE-OF-A-KIND STATIONERY WITH ENVELOPES

## *continued*

letters by hand. Or if you write a letter on the computer, you can print the letter on any sheet of stationery you like. Just remember to leave a wide margin at the top of your letter so that, when you print it, there's enough room for your letterhead design.

### WORD WIZARDRY

A "point" of type is very small. It measures 72 points per inch (or 2.5 centimeters) of type, both up and down. In the regular text of books, newspapers, and magazines, you'll usually see a standard size of 9, 10, or 11 points.

### *Here's how to make artistic and fun envelopes:*

All you have to do is save a few of your favorite magazines and maybe some old travel brochures.

### *Here's what you need:*

*A plain envelope that has a size and shape you like*
*Paper or graph paper*
*A pencil*
*A ruler*
*Scissors*
*Household glue or school paste*
*Old magazines or travel brochures*
*White stick-on labels*

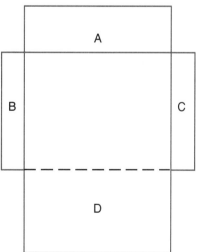

·······

# CREATE ONE-OF-A-KIND STATIONERY WITH ENVELOPES

## *continued*

### *Here's one way to make your own one-of-a-kind envelopes:*

1. Find an envelope that is the same size and shape as the one-of-a-kind envelope you wish to make. Carefully take the envelope apart and open it. That's your model envelope.

2. Use paper or graph paper to make an envelope just for practice. Use a pencil to trace around the model envelope, and carefully cut out the shape. Then fold in the flaps. Use a ruler to help make the folds crisp and sharp. With household glue or school paste, glue the bottom and side flaps (*B, C,* and *D* in the diagram). Leave the top one open (*A* in the diagram), so you can put something inside later.

3. Cut out your favorite pictures from old magazines and travel brochures. Make sure you choose pictures that are on solid, thick paper. Then cut, fold, and glue them just as you did for the practice envelope. You can use one picture, or else glue together several pictures.

   You may find it easier to make the envelope if you glue the pictures onto a piece of white paper first.

4. Use a white stick-on label to write the address. Then fill your special envelopes with letters and artwork.

### WORD WIZARDRY

People always say, "You can't tell a book by its cover." See if you can change their minds by showing them how to tell a letter by its envelope.

········
# MAKE A FINE SIGN
· · · · · · · · · · · · · · · · · · · ·

**M**aybe you'd have more than one use for a banner that says WELCOME! or CONGRATULATIONS! or HAPPY BIRTHDAY! Here's a way to make something so good that it'll work for any special occasion.

### Here's what you need:

*Felt squares, in colors and sizes you choose*

*Scrap paper*

*A pencil or chalk*

*A dark marker*

*Squeezable T-shirt, puffy, or fluorescent fabric paints, in colors you choose*

*A small wet sponge or cloth*

*Clear or fabric tape*

### Here's what you do:

1. Decide how many squares of felt you need: one for each letter in the sign, plus one for each space between words. Line up the squares, and decide what looks best. Perhaps you want your banner all one color, or two or three.

2. Practice drawing your message on scrap paper. This is a good chance to practice your sense of design. Make sure that you think about big, fat, bold letters.

3. Then use chalk or pencil to draw in each big letter on a felt square. Do it right in the middle of the square.

4. When you have the letters the way you want them, outline them with a dark marker.

5. Now fill in with fabric paint, T-shirt paint, or puffy paint. Before you begin painting, squeeze some of the paint onto a piece of scrap paper, so that you know the paint is going to flow freely. Keep a small wet sponge or cloth handy in case you want to wipe off a mistake. When you're finished, let the paint dry for several minutes.

6. Tape together the felt squares so that they spell out your message.

### WORD WIZARDRY

If you want a paper banner instead, you can use a personal computer and a color printer to make your design. Most PCs will have at least some of the type and art you want.

## PRODUCE AND BIND A BOOK

**H**ere's how to produce a book all on your own. It can be a small book, with just a few pages. Or you can experiment to see how many pages you can produce. Then you can create a special cover for your book.

### Here are decisions to make about your book:

1. Decide how large you want the pages of your book to be, and decide what shape you want. You may want to fold and measure scrap paper until you decide what size looks best.

*Hint: If you fold an ordinary 8¹/₂-by-11-inch sheet of paper into quarters, you'll have the beginnings of a small book. Each page would be 4¹/₄ by 5¹/₂ inches (about 11 by 14 centimeters).*

2. Decide what sort of paper you want for the pages of your book. Decide the color, the thickness, and how glossy you want the paper.

*Hint: You may want to experiment with mixing different kinds of paper. You may want a variety of colors or textures. Some artists like to alternate pages of different kinds of paper.*

3. Decide what sort of paper you want for the cover of your book. You may want the cover paper to be thicker and heavier than the pages. You may want a contrasting color.

### Here's what you need, besides plenty of paper and scrap paper:

*A ruler*

*A craft knife or letter opener*

*A pencil*

*Scissors*

### Here's how to produce your book:

1. Experiment folding scrap paper until you feel confident about folding the pages for your book. Fold the paper with the help of a ruler, so that the folds will be sharp and crisp. Put your pages together, so that you're sure they're lined up right, especially if you are using different papers.

2. Use a craft knife or letter opener to slit the paper at the top (or bottom) of the pages, so that the book will open the way you want it. At this point, the only fold should be at the center (spine) of the book.

   *Caution: You need adult help whenever you use a craft knife.*

. . . . . . . .
# PRODUCE AND BIND A BOOK
## *continued*

SPINE

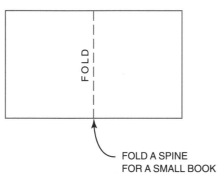

FOLD A SPINE
FOR A SMALL BOOK

**4.** If your book has fewer than four pages, measure the exact center of the cover. That's the spine, where the pages will fit. Mark the line lightly with pencil.

**5.** If your book has more than four pages, you will need to measure and mark for a wider spine. Perhaps your spine will be a fraction of an inch or just a centimeter or two wide but it needs to be wide enough so that all the pages can fit in it. Mark the two lines lightly with pencil.

SPINE FOR A
LARGE BOOK

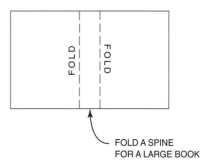

FOLD A SPINE
FOR A LARGE BOOK

**3.** Measure paper for the book cover. The cover should be the same height as the pages. But it should be three times the width of the pages. If your pages are 4$^1$/$_4$ by 5$^1$/$_2$ inches (11 by 14 centimeters), then measure a cover that is 4$^1$/$_4$ inches (11 centimeters) by 17 inches (43 centimeters). You may want to experiment with scrap paper first.

· · · · · · · ·
# PRODUCE AND BIND A BOOK
## *continued*

**6.** Use scissors or a craft knife to cut the cover to the right measure. Then fold the one or two lines of the spine. Use a ruler to make the folds sharp and crisp.

**7.** Match the center fold of your pages against the spine of the cover. Fold in the flaps of the front and back of the cover around the first and last pages of the book. Use a ruler to make sharp folds.

**8.** Now go on to bind your book.

### WORD WIZARDRY

Of course, you may want to write and illustrate your book. But a handmade book does not necessarily need writing or printing in it. Some artists produce a book to show off colors, various kinds of paper, or fancy binding.

**B**efore you produce a book, you need to plan how to put it together, plain or fancy. You may simply want to staple a short book. You may decide to sew your book together. Or you may want to tie it together with colorful yarn or ribbon.

### *Here are the three ways to bind your book:*

#### One

If you're producing a very small book, you can staple it together. Open the book out flat. Staple along the center spine of the book so that the sharp points of the staples are on the inside.

#### Two

**1.** If you're producing a longer book, you can sew it together with embroidery thread. At the center fold of the book, make holes for the thread.

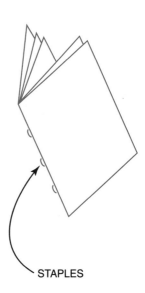

STAPLES

· · · · · · · ·
# PRODUCE AND BIND A BOOK
## *continued*

Use a needle, a drawing compass, or a paper punch to make the holes. You must use an odd number, such as three or five, and the holes should be evenly spaced.

2. Thread a needle with embroidery thread. Use double thread, and tie a knot on the end.

> :
> : *Caution: You need an adult*
> : *to help you with sewing,*
> : *especially if this is the first*
> : *time you've tried it. You'll*
> : *also need to be very careful*
> : *to avoid tearing the paper.*

3. Pull the needle through the center hole from the inside of the book toward the outside. Return the needle from the outside through the top hole. Pass over the center hole, and pull the thread through the bottom hole. You're

sewing in an S shape, back and forth. When you finish, tie the loose end with a knot.

**Three**

1. You can make the binding part of the decoration of the book by using yarn, ribbon, or gift-wrapping cord.

2. Use a paper punch to make the holes along the spine of the book. The holes should be evenly spaced along the spine. Use an even number, such as two or four.

3. Pull the yarn, ribbon, or cord through two holes. If you have more than two holes, pull another strand through the next two. Then tie the yarn, ribbon, or cord on the outside of the spine.

### WORD WIZARDRY

One way to look at a book is as an artistic creation, rather than just something to read. The earliest books were all unique productions, artistic and expensive. Now books are mass-produced, with computers, printing presses, and binding machines. But look at a display in a library or bookstore—you'll see how much creative and artistic design can still go into making a book look like a work of art.

# 5. MAKE YOURSELF A MEDIA WIZARD

*A*round the world today, people use about 3,000 separate languages, and the ways to use them are multiplying fast.

You can listen to a Spanish CD in New York, or look at tomorrow's Chinese newspapers on the Internet while you sit at a desk in Winnipeg. Ads for brand-name sneakers and soft drinks flash on TVs and neon billboards in every city in the world. Walk down a street in Nashville, Paris, or Mexico City, and you'll be seeing and hearing hundreds of messages at once, some of them not much different from the ones at home.

Ways to communicate seem to be growing, changing, and combining all at the same time.

Have a look at how all of that works. You're already a Word Wizard, so becoming a Media Wizard ought to be fun, too.

········
# BREAK INTO ADVERTISING
· · · · · · · · · · · · · · · · · · ·

**L**ook back at page 15. What's there is almost the perfect toy, and maybe the name you invented for it is close to perfect too.

But imagine now that you have a new job to do. You've decided to go into business selling the toy, and you need a way to advertise how good it is. Customers won't just show up at your store by magic. They need good reasons to come looking for your toy.

So the real focus for your advertising has to be the *customer*. There's no point in advertising unless customers learn why buying the toy will be a good move for them.

Show them why.

### Here's what you need:

*One or two old catalogs from toy stores*
*Scissors*
*Tape*
*Scrap paper*
*Colored pencils*

### Here's what you do:

1. Take a thoughtful look at how the catalogs present toys. Ask yourself some questions:

   • What's more important in the catalogs? Is it the pictures of the toys, the words in the headlines, or the words describing the toys?

   • If you think one toy seems better than others, why do you have that opinion? Is it just the toy itself, the price, or something convincing in the ad?

   • Yes or no: Do the catalogs make you want to buy toys?

2. Select the one ad you think is best, cut it out, and tape it onto a sheet of paper. Do the same with the one you think is worst.

. . . . . . . .

# BREAK INTO ADVERTISING

## *continued*

Then make a quick, small sketch of your toy and slide it around on both of the cut-out ads. Pay close attention to what seems to happen.

- Could the look of the best ad be good for your toy, or do you need something much different? Do you need more words to explain what your toy does? If so, how can you fit them in? Can you make the headline talk directly to the customer?

- What's really wrong with the worst ad? Bad art? Boring or confusing words? No idea about what a little kid would do with the toy? No good reason to buy?

3. In the space below the taped-down ads, sketch in a few first ideas for your own ad. And remember: You're not imitating the catalog ads; you're trying to do better.

Write down any headlines or other words that come to you. As soon as you get bored, put the sheets away for a while, even for a day or two.

4. When you come back to them, you may find that brand-new, much better ideas suddenly pop up. Ads can sometimes work like poems, stories, or jokes. They take on lives of their own in your mind, so you suddenly see how new versions could work. So try again, with new words and new art.

5. Once you have something definitely good on paper, do just one more thing before you make your finished color drawing. Remember that a good ad is

- not a picture plus some words,

- but a combination that speaks right to the customer,

- with a good reason to buy.

If you put enough imagination into your work here, you may be surprised by how much a simple ad can say. In just a small space, you can show people what something is, how it works, why it's different, what it will do for them, how much it costs, and where to get it.

### WORD WIZARDRY

Weak words in toy ads: *new, unique, amazing, fun, pretty, perfect.* Possibly better words for your ad: *squeeze, safe, over and over, hug, love, learn.*

## . . . . . . . .
# CUT THROUGH THE CLUTTER
. . . . . . . . . . . . . . . . . . . .

**I**n the main hallway at school, you probably have a big bulletin board covered with all kinds of schedules, announcements, art displays, photos, lists, and posters.

But when you walk by, you're not too likely to notice any one of them standing out from all the others. At a glance, the bulletin board just looks like a big complicated blur.

The same thing happens in both TV and radio, because so many images, ads, and sounds pile up on one another at once. TV and radio are cluttered, too, just like the bulletin board.

So getting attention for any one message does take creativity. Exactly the right words have to be used. They have to be clear and strong enough to be noticed and then remembered.

Think for a minute about the next Science Fair or Art Exhibit coming up at school. If you'd like more people to know about it and attend, maybe you should consider putting together an ad that could run on local radio.

If asked, many radio stations will use school announcements. And if you give them a good one, they may well broadcast it many times.

## CUT THROUGH THE CLUTTER
### *continued*

### *Here's what you need:*

*Help from a teacher*

*At least one student friend to help*

*Permission to use a good tape recorder and microphone*

*Three blank audiotape cassettes*

*A watch that shows seconds*

*Paper and pencil*

### *Here's what you do:*

1. Talk to the teacher who is running the event you think should be advertised. Tell her that most radio stations have time reserved each day for short Public Service Announcements (PSAs) about local events. Ask her to call a local station or two to see whether they'd be interested in having a 10- or 15-second announcement produced by students. Because student voices would be so unusual on the radio, you'll probably find that the station will agree to run your announcement at least once.

2. Once you have an agreement, this kind of work gets to be fun. Sit down with your paper and pencil and start thinking about your announcement. Ask yourself the same questions you would for any ad:

   • Why should people take the trouble to go to the event? What will *they* get out of it?

   • What's special about the event?

   • When is it and where is it?
   Make some quick notes on each point, but don't try to write the announcement yet.

3. Think about how you and your friend listen to the radio yourselves. Can you remember an ad or announcement that stood out somehow? What made you notice it?

   • Short, clear sentences, or longer ones?

   • A joke in it, an unusual voice, repetition, or good details?

4. Once you've thought about how radio language works, try writing out a few ideas. For a Science Fair, maybe something like this could give you a start:
   *See a box full of hungry termites. See the egg too strong to break. And see 50 other weird things at the Science Fair, 7:00 P.M. this Friday, at the First Street Middle School. The Science Fair: Be there. 7:00 P.M. Friday.*

5. When you have a rough version of your announcement, read it aloud and use the watch to time it. The sample above takes about 10 to 15 seconds, just right for radio. As you keep working on the writing, think about using two voices for the announcement, with you and

· · · · · · · ·

# CUT THROUGH THE CLUTTER

### *continued*

your friend reading different parts. Time that way of doing it, too.

6. Act out your final version for the teacher, then ask for the tape recorder to make two or three cassette copies. Look at "Report Live, from Center Court" on page 108 to make sure you know how to handle the microphone.

Record your announcement several times, until you're sure you've made it as good and as clear as you can. You'll need three copies, two for the station and one for yourself.

A small bonus for doing the work here is that you and your friend will probably get to deliver the tapes to the station. When you're there, ask somebody to give you a quick tour. Most radio people are happy to do that for students.

### WORD WIZARDRY

West of the Mississippi River, the call letters for all U.S. radio stations start with the letter *K*. To the east, they all start with *W*, except for KDKA in Pittsburgh. Reason: KDKA had the first powerful transmitter, and nobody had yet thought up a system for names.

# GET STORIES IN SHAPE FOR THE RADIO NEWS

**I**f you listen to enough radio, you've probably noticed that almost all news stories get only a few seconds. All you hear is three or four short sentences, generally with no explanation of why the story is important.

Some people get irritated about that. They think that radio news isn't worth much because it delivers so little detail. But there are good reasons for making radio news short. Here are two:

- Nearly all listeners are busy doing something else while the radio's on.
- During the morning and evening "drive times," many listeners are in cars.

So to get attention, radio news has to be a bit like commercials. Stories have to start, make a main point clearly, and then stop before the audience gets distracted again.

Good radio writers and reporters know exactly how to get a story down to the basics. To see what they do, think about doing some editing work on a story yourself.

### Here's what you need:

*A copy of your local newspaper*
*Scissors*
*Tape*
*A watch with a second hand*
*A tablet*
*Two pencils, one colored and
  one regular*

### Here's what you do:

1. Look through the paper for a story at least five or six paragraphs long. Choose one that strikes you as a typical newspaper story, maybe about a fire, a serious accident, or a local politician's speech. Or, if you like, just use this story.

*Representative Emily Sherman said Thursday that new federal guidelines will soon require six local businesses to speed up pollution-control work.*

*Speaking before 300 at the city's "Earth First" event, Sherman said that Acme Manufacturing is likely to face the biggest job.*

*"Four of the Acme plants don't even comply with current regulations," Sherman said. "Now they're being told to do more, and do it faster. They need to understand that the goal is cleaner air."*

*Asked late Thursday for a reaction, Acme spokesperson Amber Kontny questioned whether "this latest change in the rules" is realistic. "We're doing as much as we can already," Kontny said. "Reducing emissions*

........
# GET STORIES IN SHAPE FOR THE RADIO NEWS
## *continued*

*is too hard and too expensive to happen overnight."*

*Mayor Scott DeSantis also joined the debate, reminding the "Earth First" gathering that Acme's local workforce of 1,950 could face layoffs if stricter regulations ultimately force plant closings.*

*Representative Sherman concluded her remarks by appealing directly to Acme employees in the crowd. "You and your children live here and breathe the air," she said. "Don't cave in to the argument that cleaning it up is too expensive. Your health is more important than Acme's profits."*

2. If you're using this sample story, read it aloud and time it. It will probably use up a bit more than 60 seconds.

**or**

If you found your own story in a newspaper, cut it out and tape it onto a tablet page. Then read it aloud and use your watch to see how long that takes.

3. Now look back at the story you've chosen and ask yourself four questions.
   - Basically, what does this story mean?
   - Could a radio listener get almost the same meaning without hearing all the details?

   - Which details are most important, and which least?
   - Can you rewrite the story to fit into three or four sentences without changing its basic meaning?

4. Go over the story with your colored pencil and highlight *only* the details you think are most important. Then think about what they have to do with one another. That will give you a story line.

   Then decide how your radio version should start. Is there one detail that's best, and can you get it into a short, easy-to-hear sentence? Work on it until you can write down a good one, then go back to your colored underlinings. Which two or three of those should come next, to work with your first sentence?

5. As you keep rewriting, remember that your new version is for listeners, not readers. It needs

· · · · · · · ·
# GET STORIES IN SHAPE FOR THE RADIO NEWS
### *continued*

to be totally clear, and easy for an announcer to say aloud. Try reading your work aloud, to see if that makes new, simpler ideas occur to you. Eventually, maybe you'll have something like this, only better:

*"You and your children live here and breathe the air. Your health is more important than Acme's profits."*

*That was Representative Emily Sherman at yesterday's "Earth First" rally. Acme Manufacturing and five other local firms now face new deadlines to meet pollution-control regulations. (14 seconds)*

What do you think? Is your own radio story better or worse than the original print version? Or is it just different, because it's designed for listeners?

If you could get news only from radio, how much would you miss? Would you ever be getting enough information to understand all sides of a story?

### WORD WIZARDRY

Reporters for radio and TV are always looking to get "sound bites" when they do interviews. "Sound bites" are the short, colorful statements that can work to summarize a story. But they can also mislead you, because they can make the news artificially simple.

# HELP PEOPLE GET UN-LOST

**"H**ey, why don't we move the TV over to the east side of the room?"

Depending on where you live, that could be either a reasonable question or a really strange one. People in the West and Midwest often use the compass points for directions, even inside. But in the East, where both the landscapes and city streets can be confusing, what you tend to hear is "over there," "that way," or "turn right."

That's partly because so many street signs and road signs don't help much. You probably see one or two every day that ought to be clearer, bigger, or repositioned.

Talk to your teacher and friends about it. Maybe you can put together a class project to get a problem sign improved.

### Here's what you need:

*A not-very-good road sign that's somewhere close by*

*A project group of people good at math and art*

*Help from a parent or teacher*

*A disposable camera*

*Two clipboards*

*A watch that shows seconds*

*Pencils for everybody in the group*

*Sheets of paper for note-taking and sketching*

*One large piece of poster board*

*A set of colored pens and markers*

*Tape or glue*

### Here's what you do:

1. Get your group and equipment together, and go out to see the sign you think could be better.

   First, put two people in charge of photography. They need to take four photos of the sign:

   - A close-up, so that the sign fills up the whole photo.

   - A shot from 50 yards (or 50 meters) away.

## . . . . . . . .
# HELP PEOPLE GET UN-LOST
### *continued*

- Another shot, this time from 100 yards (or 100 meters) away.
- A final shot from 150 yards (or 150 meters) away.

**2.** Put two people in charge of math. Give them one clipboard and the watch, and have them go with the photographers to the 50-, 100-, and 150-yard spots.

While the photos are being shot, the math people should use the watch to time passing cars. How long does it take cars to get from each of the three spots to the sign? The answers will be in seconds. Make sure each one gets noted down on the clipboard.

**3.** At the same time, have two people work as artists. Give them the other clipboard, so they can sketch some totally new looks for the sign. Could it be shaped differently, use different colors, or be a different size?

**4.** When everybody's working, look at the surroundings of the sign yourself. Is there a better *place* it could be? Do trees, poles, or buildings make it hard to see? Sketch any new ideas you get.

**5.** Once all are done with their work, talk it over. You may all be able to agree right away on what the real problems are with the sign, and maybe even what the solution is. But don't assume that your first idea is the best one. Wait a few days until you can get the photos developed.

**6.** Then reconvene your group. Tape or glue your four photos onto the poster board so they look like this. Leave space at the top and to the right, because your math and art people will need to do some work there.

# HELP PEOPLE GET UN-LOST

## *continued*

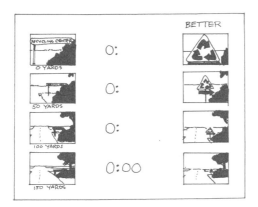

**7.** Have everybody look at the photos, going from bottom to top, to see how the sign appears as drivers approach it. Then tell the math people to pencil in the "Time" column, starting with "0:00" next to the bottom photo. From their notes, they need to show how long it takes for a car to start at 150 yards, then go to 100, 50, and 0.

At the right, under "Better," have your artists sketch in four copies of their best-looking sign. They need to show how their design would look from the four distances.

When everything looks correct, have the artists go over the whole poster, to color in all the words and numbers you're using. Then think up a good headline for the poster. What you'll have is a complete and clear idea for replacing a problem sign.

The only question then is what you do with the poster. Ask parents or a teacher to put you in touch with the local government department that handles road signs. Then go visit that office and show them your work. If your idea is a good one, they might very well agree to make the changes you're suggesting. Sign changes often happen that way.

### WORD WIZARDRY

Drivers from Boston will tell you that they go "down" to Maine, even though the whole trip heads northeast. At least six explanations exist for why Maine is "down," none of them very good.

# PUT SOME STYLE INTO A SIGN

**A**sk most people to think of *where* they've seen a good ad, and they will probably mention TV first. Some will also tell you about ads they've seen in magazines or newspapers, on posters, or even on the Internet.

But not many will mention the one place for advertising that can be just as important: the sign that stands right outside a business, showing what it is and where it is.

If you did the "Help People Get Un-Lost" project on page 103, you know that a good sign is the right size, is in exactly the most visible spot, and uses clear words and symbols. The same is true for business signs, but there's an extra need: Businesses use their signs to advertise; they want people to get more than just information from a sign.

Think about the toy you named on page 15 and advertised on page 95. What if you ran a store selling that toy and 50 others just as unique, creative, and attractive? Your store would need a great sign, something way past TOYS.

To design it, there'd be some interesting work to do.

### Here's what you need:

*Plenty of sketch paper*
*A set of colored pens or pencils*
*A ruler*
*Scissors*

### Here's what you do:

**1.** Use the ruler to draw a basic picture of the front of your store. Turn your paper sideways, so that you have enough room to make the store about 3 inches (8 centimeters) tall and 8 inches (20 centimeters) wide.

. . . . . . . .
# PUT SOME STYLE INTO A SIGN
## *continued*

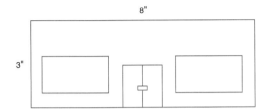

Then draw in the door and the two big windows, and spend a minute looking at the sketch.

2. Think about what you have here. It's a simple storefront, and your sign could be almost anywhere: over the door, in one or both windows, on the roof, or sticking straight out from the building.

   What's the best place? Think about it, because you want people to see it whether they're walking or driving past.

3. When you've decided on a place, think about how big and what shape the sign can be. Go to another sheet of paper and sketch various sizes and shapes that might look good. Then cut them out and spend time moving each one around on the storefront sketch. Keep an open mind, because you want new and unusual

ideas to develop while you experiment.

4. Now think about the other big need for the sign. What's on it?

   • Just words, or a picture and words? Or just a picture, with no words?

   • How much will fit inside the size and shape you like?

   • What colors will get the most attention?

   And most important, will someone glancing at your sign for half a second get a strong hint about what's in your store? Does the whole look of the sign *mean* "unusual toys"?

   Take your time at this stage, and experiment with as many different ideas as you can.

5. When you have two or three sign ideas that you really like, do finished versions of them. By now, you may even have new shapes to move around on the storefront.

   If you like this kind of work, look at page 172, too. You can find out about glyphs there, an odd sort of art that makes simple signs stand for complicated ideas.

## WORD WIZARDRY

Think about your cap, shirt, or jacket. Are you a walking sign for some team or designer?

## REPORT LIVE, FROM CENTER COURT

**A**t one time or another, almost everybody who likes sports has imagined being an announcer.

For baseball, there's the "deep, *deep* drive to right, going, going, and *gone*!" Basketball has "fakes right, goes left, and *jams*!" Golf may be quieter, but there's still the "difficult lie here, a good 160 over water into the green."

Every sport has its own odd language. Soccer matches get played on the "pitch," with "nil-nil" the score until there's a "*Gooooooooooooooooal!*"

Sports language mixes jargon, exactness, and excitement, all blended to convey the feel of the game being played. Good announcers use all three but don't try to overpower the game with too much comment. "The game's the point," they say, "not the announcer."

They also say that starting young is important, because school sports provide so many chances to work as a public-address (PA) announcer. If your school has a basketball team, a set of public-address speakers, and a microphone, the basics are all there for you to get your start as an announcer. You can announce an elementary or middle school game—or maybe even a high school game.

. . . . . . . .
# REPORT LIVE, FROM CENTER COURT
## *continued*

### *Here's what you need:*

*Before basketball season, agreements with the school coach and one teacher*

*Also before the season, two chances to practice with the microphone and speakers*

### *Here's what you do:*

1. Talk to the coach, to see if it's OK to bring in the school's PA equipment for the boys' or girls' games. Volunteer to carry the equipment in and out yourself, promise to be careful with it, and remind the coach that having the games announced will make them more fun for everybody.

2. Tell a teacher what you're planning, and ask for a demonstration of how to set up the speakers and the microphone. Make sure you understand where to put the speakers in the gym, how to plug in the microphone and volume control, and how to *double-check that all the wiring is safe.*

3. Then start planning how you'll do the announcing.

   Make a clear, easy-to-read list of what a PA announcer needs to say before and during a basketball game. It can't be too long, because your announcements need to help the crowd understand the game without being too frequent.

   Try these items to start your list:
   - The names of the two teams
   - The names and numbers for each team's starting lineup
   - The name and number of each substitute who enters the game
   - The score at the end of each quarter

4. Once you have a basic list, find a private place to rehearse exactly what you'll say during a real game. Imagine that game step by step, use your list, and remember that you're just announcing the basic facts, in very few words each time.

   Then think about adding a few items to your list. Could you name each player who scores or commits a foul, just after it happens? Are you sure you'll be able to keep track of everything as a game starts moving quickly?

5. When you have some confidence in your list, ask permission to set up the PA equipment in the gym at a time when nobody's around. Then announce the imaginary game again, to get used to how it feels to have your own voice suddenly booming out of speakers.

· · · · · · · ·

# REPORT LIVE, FROM CENTER COURT
## *continued*

You'll learn something right away about PA announcing, because the speakers will make your voice echo. It will sound almost like two voices at once. You'll have to concentrate on speaking into the microphone, and learn to ignore the echo.

6. A few days later, rehearse again with the equipment. Announce the imaginary game again, and pay attention to how you handle the microphone. You need to have it about 2 inches (5 centimeters) in front of your mouth, and switch it on only when you're going to say something.

Switch it off as soon as you're done, so that you don't end up broadcasting your breathing or other noise that will be around you at a real game.

Now you're ready. On the day of the first real game, make sure to get to the gym as early as you can. You need to set up your equipment. *Make sure nobody in the crowd will trip over the wiring.* Ask scorekeepers (or coaches or team captains) for a list of the players' names and numbers. Keep your list handy.

### WORD WIZARDRY

Then suddenly, it'll be time. With all the work you've done to prepare, you won't have any problem at all saying, "Welcome to today's game . . ."

·······
# PUT PLAIN ENGLISH INTO PRINT
· · · · · · · · · · · · · · · · · · · ·

Take a look at the front-page stories in your local newspaper. You may not find a spelling or grammatical error right away, but if you check the page several days in a row, you probably will.

You'll also find that the paper tends to use particularly strange kinds of sentences over and over, no matter what the story. Look for a few like these:

- Congress today retreated from a bipartisan pledge to complete its review of Medicare-eligibility guidelines before the long summer recess.
- Occupants of the second vehicle, traveling west on Fifty-fourth Street, also suffered multiple injuries as a result of the impact, police spokeswoman Mary P. Lancelotta said.
- Surfacing for just the second time during their June-long swoon, the Red Sox used a balk and a dramatic Joe Allen pinch-hit homer to overtake Detroit in ten innings Tuesday, 7–6, before 28,756 at Fenway Park.

Ouch. Reporters and editors do try their best, but having to publish every day often means working in a hurry. Mistakes, odd writing habits, and newspaper jargon all creep in, crowding out the plain English that could explain the facts more clearly.

If your teacher is interested, maybe you could start a class project to write to the local paper's editor and suggest improvements.

. . . . . . . .

# PUT PLAIN ENGLISH INTO PRINT
## *continued*

### *Here's what you need:*

*Five recent copies of the newspaper*

*A project group of five classmates*

*Scissors*

*Transparent tape*

*Four clean sheets of paper*

*The use of a computer or typewriter, to send a one-page letter*

### *Here's what you do:*

1. Give one copy of the paper to each student in the project group. Ask each to take the paper home and spend an hour checking through it carefully. Group members should look for any

   • spelling errors,

   • grammatical errors, or

   • sentences as hard to read as the three samples shown on page 111.

   Ask them to mark what they find and to bring the papers back to school.

2. As soon as you have time to discuss the project at school, have your teacher join the team to look over the spelling and grammatical errors found.

   After agreeing on which one is the most obvious spelling error,

and which one is the clearest grammatical mistake, cut out the stories in which they appeared.

3. Do the same for the awkward, hard-to-read sentences that were found. Since the group may have trouble agreeing on which sentence is really the hardest, read each one aloud as a test. If there's one sentence that most of you can't recite smoothly, it will probably be the winner.

4. Tape each cut-out story to a separate sheet of paper, with space left to one side. For the spelling-error sheet, use the space to write in the spelling that you all agree is correct. Do the same for the grammatical-error sheet, and write in the whole corrected sentence.

5. Take a little more time with the awkward-sentence sheet, because you need to rewrite the sentence to be clearer, but *without changing its meaning.* Ask everyone in the group to suggest different versions, then read each one aloud to help with deciding which one is best.

· · · · · · · ·
# PUT PLAIN ENGLISH INTO PRINT
## *continued*

As you'll all see, rewriting newspaper sentences is not particularly easy.

Once you have the three sheets finished, ask the group to look at this sample letter. Is it what you want to say to the newspaper's editor when you mail in your sheets? Or do you think it could use some rewriting?

> **Dear Editor,**
>
> At our school, we work every day on learning to use English well.
>
> This week, we have been reading your newspaper. We think that you usually do a good job of covering the news, but we've also found that several of your recent stories contain simple errors that could have been fixed before publication. Three of them appear on the sheets enclosed, with our own suggestions for improvements.
>
> When you have the time to look over our ideas, we would be happy to hear what you think.
>
> Sincerely,<br>[The name of your class and school]

## WORD WIZARDRY

| Odd Newspaper Words | Actual Meaning |
| --- | --- |
| New Stadium *Eyed* | New Stadium [being discussed] |
| *GOP Conclave* Starts | [Republican Party] [Meeting] Starts |
| *Dow* up 25 | [New York Stock Market Average] up 25 |
| Yankees *Decimated by DL Woes* | Yankees [have many injured players] |

## TELL YOUR STORY ON A BOARD

HERO

GENIUS

BRUNO: THE WONDER DOG!

FIRESTORM? NO PROBLEM

POUND OF HAMBURGER? NO PROBLEM.

"BRUNO"... AT THEATERS EVERYWHERE

Maybe you'd want to see Bruno's movie, and maybe not. But look at how that commercial for it is put together. The words and pictures work like a comic book, giving you a fast tour of Bruno's weird world.

The commercial is laid out as a storyboard. It *shows* you why you might be interested, with a story.

Telling a story is often the best way of getting attention for an idea. Think about a school team that needs players, a school club that's starting a new activity, or a community group that's organizing an antilitter campaign. What could a storyboard do for them? What if you designed a whole story in words and pictures, and then made big copies of it?

Try it out.

## TELL YOUR STORY ON A BOARD
### *continued*

### *Here's what you need:*

*A friend to help*

*Three large pieces of white poster board, at least 20 by 24 inches*

*A yardstick or long ruler*

*A supply of white drawing paper*

*Scrap paper*

*A set of colored pencils and markers*

*A large art eraser*

*Scissors*

*Permission to use a copy machine*

*Art glue or rubber cement*

### *Here's what you do:*

**1.** Look at this blank version of a storyboard. You can use it to get started.

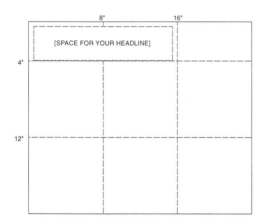

First, use your long ruler to make light, erasable pencil lines on one of the poster boards. If your board is 20 by 24 inches, go down to 4 and 12 inches to draw your horizontal lines.

Draw the two vertical lines from the points at 8 and 16 inches along the top.

That will make your board into a grid with three rows. The narrow one at the top is for your headline. The two fatter ones below it are for your drawings and words.

**2.** Now look at the two fat rows and make some decisions with your friend. Six separate spaces are there, each one big enough for one drawing or two. Can you tell your story by using just 6 pictures plus the right words, or would 12 be better? Think about it, because you need creative, good-looking answers to questions like these.

- Is there one drawing that could show people right away what your storyboard is about?

  Or do you want to use more than one to get them interested in the story?

- How many detailed drawings do you need to explain your subject completely? How can you use words to make each drawing mean more as the storyboard goes along?

- What do you want people to do as a result of seeing your storyboard? Can you show that clearly in the drawing, at the end?

· · · · · · · ·
# TELL YOUR STORY ON A BOARD
## *continued*

Spend plenty of time talking this over, because you'll have fun seeing how many different ways you can tell the same story with pictures and words. Think about how comic books do that, too.

3. When you have an idea you both like, cut out some pieces of scrap paper that would fit in the two lower rows. Sketch your picture ideas on them, and then slide them around on the poster board, to see how they can be arranged to tell your story best. Talk about the words while you do this, because you'll quickly see that they do just as much as the pictures.

4. Then put the scraps aside for a bit, so you can try out telling the story with words only. That will give you some new ideas and probably change your picture ideas, too. Keep working long enough to make sure you both think you've got the best possible story designed.

Talk about the headline too. It's the first and biggest thing most people will notice. What should it say to get the story going?

5. If you want just one copy of the storyboard to display, carefully pencil in all your final word and picture ideas so that they fit the spaces. Then add color to everything, especially the headline.

If you want more than one display copy, draw your final pictures on paper and use the copier to make as many as you need. Then you can cut them out and glue them to your other pieces of poster board. Finish the job on each board by writing in your words in color.

When you're done, see what all your friends think about the story-board. That will give you a good idea of how much a simple poster can do if you turn it into a story.

### WORD WIZARDRY

What image comes to your mind when you think of your favorite video-game or comic-book character? Does it look like a moving storyboard?

# 6. CREATE YOUR OWN WORD PUZZLES AND LANGUAGE GAMES

***G****ood* games don't just come in boxes. You can design games that are all your own, especially if you like puzzles. There's no limit to what can be done, even if all you have at the start is a basic game idea.

Give it a try.

· · · · · · · ·
# GET STARTED AS A PUZZLEMASTER
· · · · · · · · · · · · · · · · · · · ·

**Y**ou may have seen versions of this game before. In some versions, it's called "Word Ladders." Here's how to design your own, with a few of your own creative flourishes.

### Here's what you need:

*A pencil with a good eraser*
*Scrap paper*
*Two clean sheets of paper*
*Permission to use a copy machine*

### Here's what you do:

1. Spend a few minutes trying out this simple game. Its point is to see whether you can start with one word and then make new ones by changing one letter at a time. The clues will help you fill in the blanks.

R I C E    Always good for dinner

_ _ _ _    A runner would like to win one

_ _ _ _    Loans come with an interest ____

_ _ _ _    Scary animals

_ _ _ _    Friendlier animals

The answers are RACE, RATE, RATS, and CATS. And when you finish, you have a word completely different from the first one.

········
# GET STARTED AS A PUZZLEMASTER
## *continued*

**2.** If you'd like to design your own version, get the scrap paper and try out some short and simple words, like *SAND, CAVE,* and *TEAR.* Draw four blanks under each one, and see if you can make the new words by changing just one letter.

Then try other short words, until you have a total of eight or ten that will work for the game.

**3.** When you're happy with the full set of words, think up the hints the players will need for each blank. Be sure to make the hints short and clear enough to help players, and write them down on your scrap paper.

**4.** Then make neat copies of all your work on the clean sheets of paper. Before you go to the machine to make as many copies as you'll need for playing, review your work to make sure you have everything spelled correctly and laid out clearly.

All you need now is players. When the game is done, you might even think about showing them how you designed it.

### WORD WIZARDRY

See what happens if you try this same game with the word *READ.* Changing letters correctly can get you at least 15 new words.

# SCRAMBLE UP A PUZZLE

| W | A | L | K | D | O | W | N | T | O | W | N |
|---|---|---|---|---|---|---|---|---|---|---|---|
| O | P | L | A | Y | O | Z | A | M | P | A | A |
| R | P | E | S | R | K | E | B | L | E | R | P |
| D | S | R | K | M | X | Q | I | B | N | D | F |
| W | U | E | A | Z | S | L | K | M | T | E | O |
| I | X | A | T | H | P | R | E | J | W | X | R |
| Z | B | D | Q | L | O | C | M | R | O | E | A |
| A | M | U | K | W | R | I | T | E | B | R | N |
| R | R | I | D | E | T | Q | V | M | O | C | H |
| D | E | R | B | Z | S | E | K | A | O | I | O |
| R | A | C | E | C | B | A | X | G | K | S | U |
| Y | P | E | E | L | S | F | I | T | S | E | R |

Twenty-one things you can do after school are hidden in this puzzle, some as single words and some as phrases. See how many you can find and circle, such as *yardwork*. The words run across, up, down, backward, forward, and diagonally.

If you like scrambled puzzles, it's easy to invent one of your own. Maybe you could have fun making one based on your friends' names, or using only the words for things in plain sight in your room.

········
# SCRAMBLE UP A PUZZLE
## *continued*

### Here's what you need:

*Several sheets of graph paper and a pencil*

*Colored pencils to decorate the finished puzzle*

### Here's what you do:

1. On a sheet of graph paper, mark out a section to use as the area for your puzzle. If it's 10 or 12 squares high and 10 or 12 wide, you'll have plenty of room to work out a good puzzle.

2. Choose the first three words you want to use and write them in, putting one letter in each small box on the graph paper. Make one word read across, one up and down, and one at an angle.

3. Then look at those three words carefully. Which of their letters can also be used in new words you'd like to add? When you find good letters, write in the new words. Make sure that the new ones cross your original words, and that they read in different directions.

4. Once you get up to about 6 words, make sure to put in one or two that run backward, so you can get them done before you start to run out of options. Space will start to get tight at about 10 words, and you'll probably have to think about squeezing in some short, odd words. Consider the word *odd* itself, or others like *ax, bug,* or *oak.*

5. When you're sure that nothing more will fit, fill in the unused boxes with random letters. Check to see that the random ones don't accidentally create words you don't want.

6. Then get out the colored pencils. Maybe your finished puzzle needs a frame around it, or your signature as the creator. You might also consider circling a hard, backward-running word, so that people get the idea.

Then you're ready to try out the puzzle on a friend or a parent. Watching somebody work on it will tell you whether you made it too hard, too easy, or just right.

### WORD WIZARDRY

How did you do with the sample puzzle? Does it have 16 words plus 5 phrases in it, or more?

# UNMASK YOURSELF AS THE PUZZLER

**I**f you like the idea of a puzzle-within-a-puzzle, with a third one also hiding inside, here's a way to do it. When you're done and some of your friends have tried it, not many of them will be saying that this kind of puzzle is too easy.

### Here's what you need:

*Several sheets of graph paper and a pencil*

*A colored pencil*

### Here's what you do:

1. Look at the sketch here. It shows 100 graph-paper boxes being used, and it has "I am the puzzler" built in so that it seems to shape the letter *B*.

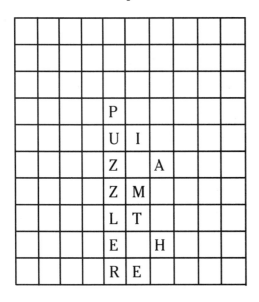

2. Do the same with a 100-box square on your own graph paper. But *use the shape of your own first initial* when you put down the letters for "I am the puzzler." That sentence can be arranged to look like any letter, so it will work for *J, A, M,* or any other initial. Try different ways of doing it until you get something that looks completely clear.

3. Then think about what you already have here. Your initial and the "puzzler" sentence mean that two related puzzles have been built in right from the start.

4. Create the third puzzle by filling in the empty boxes with words that surround and pass through "I am the puzzler." Keep a list of the words you use, and when no more will fit, fill in the empty boxes with random letters.

5. Now put the puzzle away for about ten minutes, because you need to take a fresh look at it before going on.

When you do check back on it, ask yourself just one question: Is "I am the puzzler" now so hidden that it makes the puzzle too hard to be fun? If you think so, consider using your colored

· · · · · · · ·

# UNMASK YOURSELF AS THE PUZZLER

### *continued*

pencil to circle just the "I am" part. That could work as a hint and would probably also look good if you're going to frame the puzzle in color.

**6.** Whatever you decide, go ahead and make your final, clean copy. Then you'll be ready to try out the puzzle with your friends. Tell them they need to find

- the total number of words you've hidden,
- a complete hidden sentence, and
- the clue showing who created the puzzle.

Because it's three puzzles at once, they won't find this one particularly simple. Once they've tried, you may want to show them how you did it with just 100 little boxes.

### WORD WIZARDRY

A good way to make simple crossword puzzles harder is to use puns as the clues. You can use "3.1417++" as the clue for the math term "pi," or "pi*es*," or "pi*lot*."

# TAKE ENGLISH A LITTLE *TOO* FAR

**E**nglish is one of the best languages for designing word games and puzzles, especially weird ones.

If you like the idea of odd, unpredictable games, there's a good way to set up a word puzzle that starts out easy and has just two basic rules. It does get harder as you play it, but the fun is seeing how far you and some friends can get.

### Here's what you need:

*One sheet of graph paper and a pencil, to design the game*

*Extra sheets of graph paper and pencils, for the players*

### Here's what you do:

**1.** Find five boxes in the middle of your sheet of graph paper. Write *s-t-a-r-t* in them. Then check this chart to understand the first rule of the game. It shows how players can use the letters in *start* to think up five other words that make a sentence.

| d |   |   |   | n |   |
|---|---|---|---|---|---|
| o |   |   |   | a |   |
| g |   | b | a | s |   |
| **s** | **t** | **a** | **r** | **t** |   |
|   | h | r | e | y |   |
|   | a | k |   |   |   |
|   | t |   |   |   |   |

**2.** Think about the "Do**g**s **t**hat **b**ark **a**re na**s**ty" sentence that

you see here. It may not be a great sentence, but it does meet the first rule of the game, and it could be a winner. So could "**S**top a**t a**ll **r**ed lig**h**ts," along with dozens of others.

That's why there's a second rule to this game. It says that each player is given one letter that can't ever be used in any of the five words the player invents.

**3.** Put in the two rules this way. First, write *s-t-a-r-t* on as many sheets as you'll need for the game. Then, at the top of each player's sheet, write in the one letter that can't be used. The best ones to try are probably *e, i, o,* and *u,* because having to avoid one vowel makes each player's job much harder.

**4.** When you're all prepared, just get the players together, explain both rules, and start. Anybody who can get to a five-word sentence without using the letter you've chosen is a winner.

········

# TAKE ENGLISH A LITTLE *TOO* FAR
## *continued*

This game starts to be fun when three or four players try it together. Usually someone moves out to a quick lead, but then has trouble finishing. Having to avoid one vowel while making up a five-word sentence isn't so easy.

If you want, you can make the game even harder by choosing one or two consonants that can't be used, but maybe that's going too far. Try it yourself. Adding the third rule turns this basically simple game into a very difficult one.

### WORD WIZARDRY

In 1939, Ernest Vincent Wright published *Gadsby,* a novel that didn't use the letter *e* even once. Sample sentence: "Gadsby was walking back from a visit down in Branton Hill's manufacturing district on a Saturday night."

## PLAY NYMS, GRAMS, AND DROMES

**S**ometimes the best word games are the ones you play by yourself. You can make them as easy, hard, or weird as you want, and play them whenever you have free time.

Here are three good ones, each based on one of the stranger possibilities that English words offer. Give them a try.

### Here's what you need:

*Blank pages in the back of a school tablet or notebook*

*A regular pencil with a good eraser*

### Here's what you do:

**Try Out Eponyms**

1. The first game uses *eponymous* words. That means using a person's name as a substitute for some situation or action that's totally typical of the person. For example, suppose your friend Kevin is well known as the messiest person in class. What if you started to use his name as a shorthand way to

mean "mess"? You could say:

- "Oops, I've Kevined my homework," or

- "Wow, it looks like somebody Kevinized this whole room."

2. To make a game out of eponymous words, go to the back of your notebook and make a list like this one. Once you get started, you'll probably have fun seeing how long you can make it. You can use any names, even brand names, and there's no limit to what you can pick as the situations that link to the names.

| Situation | Name |
|---|---|
| being picky about details | Mr. Fussy |
| always wanting to get out of work | _____ |
| always wearing the newest styles | _____ |
| _____ | _____ |
| _____ | _____ |
| _____ | _____ |

. . . . . . . .
# PLAY NYMS, GRAMS, AND DROMES
## *continued*

### Play Isograms

**1.** Like *eponymous, isogram* is an odd word that means something reasonably simple. In fact, *isogram* is an isogram itself, because no letter in it is used more than once. That's the only rule in an isogram game, and the challenge is to see how long a word you can make without repeating any letter.

**2.** Go to the back of your notebook and see what you can do, maybe starting with words of 5 letters. For example, *table* would work for this game, but not *books* or *seats.* Then think of 6-letter words, and keep going until you've passed 10-letter words. It gets harder then, and you'll definitely need the eraser as you go along.

See if you can beat *ambidextrously,* which uses 14 letters without any repetition.

### Put Together Palindromes

**1.** *Palindromes* are short phrases or sentences that can be read forward and backward, with no change in what they mean. The best-known example of a palindrome is probably "Madam, I'm Adam," a joke about what Adam could have said to introduce himself to Eve. Read it backward, letter by letter, and you'll see how palindromes line up.

**2.** To try it yourself, start with something simple, such as names. *Ann* doesn't work, but *Anna* does. So does *Bob.* Can you think of any more without wearing out your eraser? Then take the game a little further, into longer words and short phrases. For example, if a thing weighs less than 2,000 pounds, is there a palindrome that would describe it? How about "not a ton"?

The best way to invent your own palindromes is to write inward on your paper, working from both the left and the right, so that you're sure the repeating letters are in correct positions. Most people find that this game starts to get hard as early as the third letter, but that's the fun of it.

· · · · · · · ·
# PLAY NYMS, GRAMS, AND DROMES
## *continued*

To make it work, you have to keep changing what the palindrome is about.

### WORD WIZARDRY

Sports are full of eponymous words. In basketball, if another player blocks a shot back into your face, maybe you're "eating the Wilsonburger." In baseball, you can strike out because the pitcher "Cy Younged" you.

Eponymous words even work in reverse. The word *tawdry* refers to something sleazy and cheap. Yet the source for tawdry is Saint Audrey, because people sometimes sold poor-quality lace at fairs on her feast day. That lace became known as *sin t'Audrey lace,* then *tawdry lace,* then just *tawdry,* all very strange ways to use a saint's name.

· · · · · · · ·

# PLAY STUPID CUPID

· · · · · · · · · · · · · · · · · · · ·

**H**ere's a word game that's good to play with a friend or two if you have just a few spare minutes. You can have fun with it at lunch, while riding in a car, or during times when you're waiting for something else to start.

There's no equipment, and the rules are simple.

### Here's what you do:

**1.** Before you start, think up several pairs of words that rhyme perfectly, like the ones in the chart. Then think up good definitions for them, like these:

| Rhyming Words | Definitions |
|---|---|
| funny bunny | a rabbit onstage at the Comedy Club |
| weird beard | what happens if a man shaves only his chin |
| stupid Cupid | a dumb little angel with a bow and arrow |
| spaghetti confetti | pasta chopped into tiny pieces |
| cellar dweller | somebody who lives in a basement |
| _____ | _____ |
| _____ | _____ |
| _____ | _____ |

· · · · · · · ·
# PLAY STUPID CUPID
## *continued*

2. When you're ready to play, start by giving your friends one example. Make one of your definitions into a question, and then give them the right, rhyming answer to it. They'll catch on right away, and you'll be ready to try some more questions and see how long it takes to form the rhymes.

3. Once the game gets going, you can also think about combining questions, so that some of the rhymes already used can be put together. For instance, why would fat little angels like to hold all their parties in Italian restaurants? Because they're stupid Cupids, and they think it's fun to throw spaghetti confetti?

Have your friends make up their own questions, too. If you all take the game far enough, you can get into hundreds of rhymes.

### WORD WIZARDRY

A game like this also works for homonyms, the kinds of words that sound exactly the same but have different meanings. For example, what's a thoroughbred with a sore throat? A "hoarse horse"? What's a rock that's braver than all the others? A "bolder boulder"?

## GIVE A FRIEND A REBUS TO READ

. . . . . . . . . . . . . . . . . . .

**J**ust like this sentence, more than 99 percent of what you read every day is made up of constantly rearranged letters and numerals. Each arrangement is so exact that even if you don't understand a word or a number, you still know that you can find out. The systems behind ~~words and numbers give you a good start, no matter how complicated~~ an idea might look in writing.

But what about the other 1 percent, the things like ✓, ➜, and ✂ that you "read" every day? They aren't like words or numbers. There's no system to symbols like these, and they can look like anything from a light-bulb to a cigarette with a slash through it. Somehow you just learn them, one at a time, without any system to help you.

You can even learn something that's half-symbol and half-word, called a rebus. The idea is to use a simple drawing of one thing to stand for a word that means something else. If you string enough of these drawings together, you can get a message that shows no words but can still be read.

Maybe you'd like to try one on a friend.

### Here's what you need:

*A good friend who knows how you think*

*A plain sheet of paper*

*Three or four colored pencils*

### Here's what you do:

**1.** Look at this odd but easy way of writing "I love football."

To get it, a reader has to say "eye" out loud, then remember that the heart can mean "love."

**2.** Now look at something a bit more complicated. What do you think it could mean?

Call "mi" at 4:00, "sew" I "no" what's up?

**3.** Now think about putting together a message of your own. The chart here gives you a start by translating some useful words into pictures, and there's plenty of room left for you. Fill it up with some word-and-drawing pairs you think would be good for a rebus message to your friend.

........

# GIVE A FRIEND A REBUS TO READ
## *continued*

| Drawing | Word | Drawing | Word | Drawing | Word |
|---|---|---|---|---|---|
| ☺ | like | 〜 | fly |  | _____ |
| ☹ | don't like | 😑 | sleep |  | _____ |
| 👁 | peek |  | _____ |  | _____ |
| 🥄 | or (from oar) |  | _____ |  | _____ |
| 🏃 | run, hurry |  | _____ |  | _____ |
| 🚦 | go |  | _____ |  | _____ |

**4.** Try stringing them together into the message. Use your regular pencil at first, then think about which symbols would be better and clearer if you used color as an added hint. When you're happy with your ideas, make the finished, colored message for your friend.

Handing it over ought to be fun. You'll probably see your friend realize that the rebus is some sort of code. Watch to see what happens next, because it won't take long for the drawings to get read as words.

**WORD WIZARDRY**

# GUESS A WORD, SAVE A LIFE

"**H**angman" is a weird old game where guessing the right word prevents a hanging. If you get the word wrong, you see what can happen.

Two people or more can play the game, and it moves so fast that you can try it in about a minute.

### Here's what you need:

*At least two players*
*A blackboard, chalk, and an eraser*
*Or paper, pencil, and an eraser*

### Here's what you do:

**1.** To start the game, make a drawing that looks like this.

**2.** Think up a word with the right number of letters to fill in the blanks, but *don't* write it in. Just keep it in mind while you explain the rules.

- Players have to guess what your word is, one letter at a time, and take turns.

- If a guessed letter is not in the word, you will start drawing the hanged man. The first wrong guess means his head gets drawn. The second means the body, the third an arm, and so on.

. . . . . . . .

# GUESS A WORD, SAVE A LIFE

## *continued*

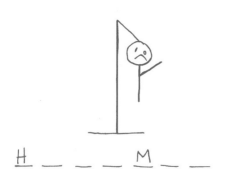

- To win the game, players have to guess your complete word before the entire body of the man gets drawn. Otherwise, he's in big trouble, and the players all lose, too.
3. Try it with five-, six-, or seven-letter words that all the players will know, and play quickly.

- If a correct letter is guessed, you will write it into the proper blank and erase one part of the man.

The cartoon man isn't in a position to wait very long for the results.

### WORD WIZARDRY

Guess the name of a TV game show. Nobody gets hanged on it, but the game is the same as this one.

. . . . . . . .
# SQUARE UP A WORD SQUARE
. . . . . . . . . . . . . . . . . . . .

**N**obody really knows, but there are probably several hundred different games that depend on moving things around inside a grid.

Ticktacktoe is a simple one. Checkers is harder, and chess can be much harder, but almost all grid games share the same basic feature: Players have to think ahead as the games go along, to try to see patterns developing that might help them win. Even in ticktacktoe, putting the first mark in the center box almost always determines how the rest of the game will go.

So strategy is important. Seeing one or two moves ahead lets you try to influence the game, so pure chance and the other players' moves don't always work against you. If you'd like to design and test an unusual game to see how strategy works, try Word Squares.

### Here's what you need:

*Six sheets of graph paper and a pencil for yourself*

*Enough pencils for one, two, or three other players*

### Here's what you do:

1. Use the lines on the paper to draw four separate squares that are five boxes high and five wide. Leave plenty of space between the squares. Then make five copies of the sheet.

2. Show one sheet to the players, give them their pencils, and explain the Word Squares rules.

   - Each player owns one of the squares you've drawn.

   - The game starts with you calling out any letter at all.

   - The others then have some choices. They can write that letter into any one of the 25 little boxes in their own squares. Or they can choose not to write it at all.

   - Then another player calls out a letter, and the players have the same choices with it.

   - The point of the game is to arrange the called-out letters into five-letter words (worth five points) and four-letter words (worth three). Words can read either horizontally or vertically, and everybody takes turns calling out letters.

3. Keep playing until nobody can make any more choices. The player with the highest score wins.

........
# SQUARE UP A WORD SQUARE
## *continued*

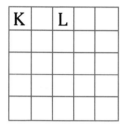 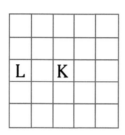 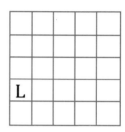 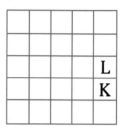

Because you made a total of six playing sheets, you can try this game several more times, so that the players get smarter about it. You'll have fun seeing which letters people tend to choose and how they try to arrange them to build the best strategy. They'll also be watching one another's squares, both to get ideas and to see what score they'll need to beat.

### WORD WIZARDRY

Instead of owning one square each, what if the players had to use two or three at once? Would they get better or worse at building strategies?

# 7. SEND SECRET MESSAGES AND CRACK MYSTERY CODES

**Y**ou really ought to learn all about how to send and receive secret messages. They're lots of fun, and you never know when they could save your life.

You may be surprised to learn that a code uses just plain, ordinary language. What's different is that the language means something other than the obvious.

During World War II, the Nazis destroyed many of the telephone lines in Britain. So the British resorted to sending their messages by radio. Some of these were ordinary messages about meetings and events and even birthday wishes, just as you might hear on your radio now. Other messages appeared normal, but were top-secret. Whenever an important secret message was about to come on, the radio broadcast an alert with this strange sentence:

He has a weird voice.

So, WHAT'S THE MESSAGE?

"GO BRUSH YOUR TEETH"

Of course, the British were no fools. So they broadcast plenty of dummy messages to mislead any of the enemy who might have figured out the code.

Ciphers are different. A cipher is a secret message written with single letters rather than whole words. Sometimes the letters of words are scrambled. If you're playing games, call that an anagram. If you're serious, call it a transposition cipher.

The other type of cipher is full of substitutions. Instead of the regular letters of the alphabet, you substitute other letters, numbers, or symbols. For example, A, B, C, and D can become 1, 2, 3, and 4—or preferably a substitute that is strange and difficult. Ciphers are especially complicated these days, since computers can be programmed to set them up, then change them repeatedly.

You'll love thinking up your own extra twists and turns to make your secret message really complicated. You can even devise the best ways to crack codes and figure out secret messages.

*Hint: When you want to work on ciphers, get out graph paper. That will help you keep things straight and logical.*

. . . . . . . .

# SCRAMBLE AND UNSCRAMBLE
# A SECRET MESSAGE

. . . . . . . . . . . . . . . . . . .

**Y**ou can buy anagram games or make up your own. You can play by yourself or with friends. You will probably want to have paper and pencil on hand, but basically you play when and where you want.

All you need to do is scramble and unscramble words. This is a transposition cipher, because you position the letters all different ways.

### Here are some game variations:

1. Give each player a word to rearrange. Don't just scramble the word at random. Scramble it so that it becomes another word. A regular word or two is best, but it's also all right for the word to be misspelled, shortened, or silly.

2. Get the players to rearrange their own names or the names of the other players. It's more fun if you can scramble the names so that they become other names— or as close as possible.

3. Scramble something you need to memorize. You'll learn fast while you're busy scrambling and unscrambling. For example, you could learn the names of states, provinces, and countries by making a list of them scrambled.

### Here are a few famous examples to try unscrambling:

1. Unscramble this sentence and you'll have the eight notes of the musical scale:

**I dream of toad oils.**

2. Unscramble these words and get the names of states and provinces:

**Fair can oil**

**Dad won lone fun**

**Taxes**

**Tear lab**

**Thank at door**

### WORD WIZARDRY

Word scrambling is fun as a game. But with long messages, and sometimes short, people often find the unscrambling slow and difficult. You need a computer to scramble and unscramble all the possible combinations. Look at how many scrambles you can make of just one word. Try a three-letter word like *has*. Then try to figure out a longer scramble.

*Hint: This is another province of Canada, and it is two words.*

S h o m b i b a c i r u t i l

*For all answers, see page 154.*

. . . . . . . .
# SEND A SECRET MESSAGE BY DESIGN
. . . . . . . . . . . . . . . . . . . .

**Y**ou can make a cipher just by putting the letters into a design. Start out with something simple, and then make it more and more complicated. That's how codes and ciphers work.

### Here's one way to put letters into a secret design:

**1.** Begin with a simple message:

**Meet me after school**

**2.** Write the message like this:

**m e m a t r c o l**
**e t e f e s h o**

All you do is put the message onto two lines. You can still read it.

**3.** Then write the lines as if they were two strange words:

**mematrocol etefesho**

Someone who tries to figure it out might spend a lot of time rearranging what look like two scrambled words. But a friend who knows the trick can figure out the message right away.

### WORD WIZARDRY

Look at the icons on a computer screen. They work as glyphs (or codes) for programs. Then those programs run on codes, sending instructions in yet more codes.

· · · · · · · ·
# SEND A SECRET MESSAGE WITH A KEY WORD
· · · · · · · · · · · · · · · · · · · · ·

**H**ere is another way to send secret messages by constructing a design. Of course, no one should know the design except you and your allies. This cipher is more complicated. Your opponents will have a hard time figuring it out.

***Here's how to put a secret message into a key-word design:***

**1.** Begin with a simple message:

### Danger: Leave area at once

**2.** Decide on a key word. This word should not use any letter more than once. And it should have nothing to do with the message. Here is a sample key word:

### Pencil

**3.** Assign a number to each letter of the key word according to where the letter appears in the alphabet. Here's how to assign numbers to the sample key word, *pencil.* The letter *c* is number one because, of these six letters, it appears first in the alphabet.

| | | |
|---|---|---|
| p | = | 6 |
| e | = | 2 |
| n | = | 5 |
| c | = | 1 |
| i | = | 3 |
| l | = | 4 |

**4.** Construct a rectangle or chart with rows and columns. Each row of the rectangle should have the same number of letters as there are in the key word. Since *pencil* has six letters, construct the sample chart with six rows across.

| P | E | N | C | I | L |
|---|---|---|---|---|---|
| | | | | | |
| | | | | | |
| | | | | | |
| | | | | | |

· · · · · · · ·
# SEND A SECRET MESSAGE WITH A KEY WORD
### *continued*

**5.** Write out the message in the rectangle. Since the sample chart has six rows, write the message with six of the letters across each row.

**6.** If you have empty spaces left in the chart, fill them in with one or two extra, meaningless letters, such as *A* or *X*. Be sure to tell your allies what the extra letter is. Codemasters call these letters nulls.

| 1 | 2 | 3 | 4 | 5 | 6 |
|---|---|---|---|---|---|
| G | A | E | R | N | D |
| V | E | E | A | A | L |
| A | E | T | O | A | R |
| X | C | X | X | E | N |

**8.** Now write the columns as rows.

|   |   |   |   |
|---|---|---|---|
| P | E | N | C | I | L |

| P | E | N | C | I | L |
|---|---|---|---|---|---|
| D | A | N | G | E | R |
| L | E | A | V | E | A |
| R | E | A | A | T | O |
| N | C | E | X | X | X |

| G | V | A | X |
|---|---|---|---|
| A | E | E | C |
| E | E | T | X |
| R | A | O | X |
| N | A | A | E |
| D | L | R | N |

**7.** Then rearrange the chart so that the columns are in order of the number you assigned to each letter. Now your message is beginning to look mysterious.

**9.** Then just write out the weird words, and send the message to your allies. How will anyone ever figure this out?

**gvax aeec eetx raox naae dlrn**

• • • • • • • •

# SEND A SECRET MESSAGE WITH A KEY WORD
## *continued*

### WORD WIZARDRY

Remind your allies of how to read your secret message. They must know the key word first, and it would help if they knew the nulls. Here are the backward steps to take:

1. Take a first look at the secret message. Put the letters into a chart.
2. Make a new chart in which you switch the columns into rows.
3. Look at the key word, and rearrange the columns so that they are in the order of the letters of the key word. If you know the nulls, block them out or erase them.

## · · · · · · · ·
# SEND A SECRET MESSAGE FROM THE PIG PEN
· · · · · · · · · · · · · · · · · · · ·

**T**his is called the Pig Pen Cipher.
That name makes it sound silly, but for hundreds of years this cipher has seen serious uses. A secret society of the Middle Ages used it. Then during the Civil War, when Union soldiers were captured by the Confederates, they used this cipher to send messages from prison.

But you can see why it's called Pig Pen when you start putting letters of the alphabet into pens.

### *Here's how to put the alphabet into pig pens:*

| ABC | DEF | GHI |
|-----|-----|-----|
| JKL | MNO | PQR |
| STU | VWX | YZ |

### *Here's how to send a secret message in the pig pen:*

**1.** Begin with a simple message:

> **Escape at midnight. Meet in woods to north.**

**2.** Look at the alphabet in its pig pens, or grid. Notice how, if you take it apart, each section of the grid has a definite shape. Write the message by drawing the shape of the pig pen in which each letter appears. Here's how the word *escape* looks with the pig-pen shape of each letter:

 E

 S

C

A

 P

 E

· · · · · · · ·

# SEND A SECRET MESSAGE FROM THE PIG PEN

### *continued*

**3.** You'll notice that some of the pig-pen shapes for the letters in *escape* are the same. Add a dot in the grid shape to show whether the letter of that grid is to the left, in the middle, or to the right. Here's how the word *escape* looks with the dots added:

Now try putting the rest of a message into the pig pens.

### WORD WIZARDRY

The codes that run computers couldn't be simpler. They're made up entirely of zeros and ones. The tricky part is that the zeros and ones repeat in complicated patterns, for thousands of lines.

# SEND A SECRET MESSAGE ALL
# THROUGH THE ALPHABET

This cipher has a long and honorable history, in war and peace. To create a cipher, you substitute another letter or a number for each letter of the alphabet.

In World War II, both the Americans and the Japanese invented ciphering machines. The basic idea for some of these machines was to hook up two of the "electronic" typewriters of the 1940s. The connection was a system of revolving disks. When you typed a letter on the first typewriter, it came out as another letter on the second typewriter.

These days, computers can do the work for you even more swiftly. And to escape the enemy's attempts to break through, these machines can change the ciphers as often as you want.

### Here's how to make up an alphabet cipher to suit yourself:

**1.** Substitute a number for each letter of the alphabet. Here's a simple way:

| a | b | c | d | e | f | g | h | i | j | k | l | m |
|---|---|---|---|---|---|---|---|---|---|---|---|---|
| 1 | 2 | 3 | 4 | 5 | 6 | 7 | 8 | 9 | 10 | 11 | 12 | 13 |

| n | o | p | q | r | s | t | u | v | w | x | y | z |
|---|---|---|---|---|---|---|---|---|---|---|---|---|
| 14 | 15 | 16 | 17 | 18 | 19 | 20 | 21 | 22 | 23 | 24 | 25 | 26 |

**2.** Substitute another letter for each letter of the alphabet. Here's an exactly backward way:

| a | b | c | d | e | f | g | h | i | j | k | l | m |
|---|---|---|---|---|---|---|---|---|---|---|---|---|
| z | y | x | w | v | u | t | s | r | q | p | o | n |

| n | o | p | q | r | s | t | u | v | w | x | y | z |
|---|---|---|---|---|---|---|---|---|---|---|---|---|
| m | l | k | j | i | h | g | f | e | d | c | b | a |

· · · · · · · ·

# SEND A SECRET MESSAGE ALL
# THROUGH THE ALPHABET

### *continued*

**3.** Try a Caesar cipher. The great emperor of ancient Rome, Julius Caesar, had a private cipher. He moved just three letters down the alphabet. Unfortunately, his enemies figured out his cipher all too quickly. Caesar had to think of another system.

But this one is still called the Caesar cipher. Here's how to substitute one letter for another one three letters down the alphabet:

| a | b | c | d | e | f | g | h | i | j | k | l | m |
|---|---|---|---|---|---|---|---|---|---|---|---|---|
| c | d | e | f | g | h | i | j | k | l | m | n | o |

| n | o | p | q | r | s | t | u | v | w | x | y | z |
|---|---|---|---|---|---|---|---|---|---|---|---|---|
| p | q | r | s | t | u | v | w | x | y | z | a | b |

**4.** Think of all the other combinations you can try. Just keep track of your latest cipher decision—you want your opponents to be confused, not you!

### WORD WIZARDRY

Here's a puzzle. Find a secret message inside this message.

**Hint:** *It's a sentence with four words in it, and it's started for you here. (If you wish, look for the full answer on page 154.)*

**W**hy **do** ra**r**e **d**iamonds **whiz ar**ound **s**o fast?
**Are** they **ve**ry nervous? You want hints here?

## SEND A HOBO'S MESSAGE

**Y**ou can always find people who live outside of ordinary society. They may be hoboes wandering from place to place. They may be homeless people on the streets of a city. They may be thieves and pickpockets. But they have their own society, and often they have their own code. They help out one another.

Imagine that an old, experienced hobo catches a ride in a boxcar to a faraway town. When he gets there, what does he do first?

He looks for messages in out-of-the-way places, maybe graffiti or marks on a fence or a walkway, where no one else would notice. What do these messages tell the hobo? To other people, they may look like meaningless scratches. But to the hobo, they say something valuable.

***Here are a few traditional hobo messages:***

**1.** Three circles for coins

**2.** A circle with an arrow through it

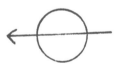

**3.** A square with a dot in it, and a wavy line underneath

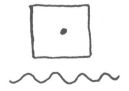

**4.** An outline of a cat

**5.** Ragged lines for teeth

**6.** A circle with a line through it, meaning a broken head

· · · · · · · ·

# SEND A HOBO'S MESSAGE

## *continued*

### *Here are meanings for the six secret hobo symbols:*

1. You may get money here (by begging, stealing, or maybe even working).
2. There's no use going this way.

3. Don't drink the water here.
4. A kindhearted woman or a woman alone lives here.
5. Beware of dog.
6. This is an easy place to rob.

See if you can come up with a secret symbol for your friends. The code may mean a name, or it can represent some more complicated message.

### WORD WIZARDRY

Until about the last 250 years, only a minority of people could read or write. All the others depended on pictures and symbols instead of written words. So the sign for an inn called the Fighting Rooster or the Golden Swan would show a picture of a fighting rooster or a golden swan. Sometimes the sign had no words on it. You can still see places that keep up the tradition, often with elaborate, artistic signs.

· · · · · · ·
# DECODE A SECRET MESSAGE
· · · · · · · · · · · · · · · · · · ·

**W**hat if you're having trouble figuring out a secret message? At first, the message looks like a mess.

### Here are ways to get started:

1. Look for the most common letter, number, or symbol that appears in the message. That may be the letter *E,* since that letter appears most frequently in English (and also in Spanish, French, and German).

2. Look for other most common letters. This method works particularly well in figuring out an anagram or scrambled message. Remember this phrase:

**Reason it.**

That one phrase contains the most frequent letters. Add *D*

and *H* and you account for more than 70 percent of the letters in English words.

3. Then look for the least common letters. This method works particularly well in figuring out a substitution cipher. These are the least frequently used letters of our alphabet:

**F, J, Q, X, Y**

4. Look for apostrophes in the secret message. They are a clue that the letter following may be *s* or *t.* (Think of words about possession, like *David's,* or contractions, like *won't.*)

........

# DECODE A SECRET MESSAGE

## *continued*

**5.** Look for words of one letter. They are probably *a* or *I*.

**6.** Look for clues to the most commonly used English words. The message probably contains some of the most commonly used words, and they are probably only two or three letters long. If you can figure them out, you have clues to figuring out the other words. These are the most frequently used words in English:

**the, of, and, a, to, in, is, you, that, it, for**

**7.** Once you've recognized a few letters and a few of the most common words, look at the shapes of the rest of the words. You may see words that seem to appear more than once, and you can begin to make sense of the others.

### WORD WIZARDRY

During wartime, every military code ever designed has been broken—except one. That was the Navajo code used by the U.S. military during World War II. Divisions, regiments, battalions, and companies were all given Navajo clan names. Ships were given fish names, and airplanes were birds.

The code also used groups of Navajo words to stand for each letter of the English alphabet. That way, English words could be spelled out if necessary. The coded messages were all broadcast and received by Navajo soldiers. They were called code talkers.

· · · · · · · ·
# SEND A CODE FOR HELP
· · · · · · · · · · · · · · · · · · · ·

**W**hat does "SOS" mean? This is a trick question. People think it means "Save Our Ship" or "Save Our Souls." It doesn't. It doesn't mean anything, other than a general call for help. It's just an easy-to-remember arrangement of the dots and dashes of Morse code. This is one code you ought to know. It could be a lifesaver.

Morse code is made up of just two signals—short and long. Altogether, the various combinations of short and long signals make up an alphabet. Or, if you're writing Morse code, it's a dot for the short signal and a dash for the long one.

You can communicate in Morse code with something as simple as a flashlight or as sophisticated as a ship-to-shore radio. Try a flashlight to practice sending an "SOS."

. . . . . . . .

# SEND A CODE FOR HELP

## *continued*

### *Here's how to call for help in Morse code:*

**• • •       — — —       • • •**

**Three dots, three dashes, three dots**
(over and over)

#### WORD WIZARDRY

Morse code is more than 100 years old. Samuel Morse invented it for use with the new telegraph machines, so that operators could transmit it easily, with short and long signals.

Now that the telegraph is out of date, you might think that Morse code is out of date, too. But the code is still in use, even with advanced technology. If you went to the U.S. Naval Academy, you'd find it's required learning. Airports use it to help guide airplanes, and you still see it marked on buoys to guide ships into the right sea channels.

And people still use dots and dashes to call for help.

·······

# Answers, Chapter 7
# Send Secret Messages and
# Crack Mystery Codes

·····················

### *Scramble and Unscramble a Secret Message:*

1. "I dream of toad oils" can unscramble into these notes of the musical scale:

**do re mi fa so la ti do.**

2. These words unscramble into these states and provinces:

**California**
**Newfoundland**
**Texas**
**Alberta**
**North Dakota**

### *Word Wizardry*

You can arrange the word *has* six ways: has, ahs, hsa, sha, sah, and ash. The random scramble is:

**British Columbia**

### *Send a Secret Message All Through the Alphabet:*

### *Word Wizardry*

The secret sentence is:

**Word wizards are everywhere.**

# 8. TALK YOUR WAY AROUND THE WORLD

**Q:**
What if you were in a tuktuk, with tumas ren and bigfella win?
**A:**
You'd be putting on your life jacket.

**Q:**
What if you saw a blooming roadtrain doing 150 klicks?
**A:**
You'd be getting out of the way, fast.

**A**nd both times, you'd also be about halfway around the world. To be in a tuktuk, you might be in Papua New Guinea, where many people don't speak your kind of English. Instead, they use Pidgin English, a peculiar language that calls a small boat a tuktuk because that's how the motor sounds.

To see a roadtrain, you might be out somewhere in the middle of Australia. Giant trucks roar down the roads there, towing three or four heavy trailers and raising huge clouds of dust.

Around the world, almost a billion people do use English every day, but not necessarily in the ways you might predict. Depending on where you go, the language can actually change enough to give you a whole set of new ways to talk.

To see how, imagine going on a really long trip.

# TALK PIDGIN, SO YOU CAN MEET A MONKEY

**L**ike every other visitor, you'll be amazed when you first arrive in Papua New Guinea.

You've come into a country with rain forests and tropical mountain ranges. You're seeing wild pigs, orchids, parrots, and bright green snakes, all in a landscape of seashores, jungles, and cliffsides.

Things sound strange, too, because people are speaking dozens of different languages, plus the version of English they call Pidgin. When you first hear it, you probably won't understand much Pidgin at all. It's only a spoken language, with no formal spelling or grammatical rules.

But it's still English, just modified so that it will work as a simplified common language and allow people from anywhere in Papua New Guinea to understand each other. It will even start to work for you after a bit.

All you have to do is imagine three things:

1. You're actually on the island.
2. You've decided to go to school there for a few days, to check things out.
3. You've run into a small problem with your homework.

### Here's what you need:

*A pencil*

### Here's what you do:

1. Imagine that one of your school days in Papua New Guinea doesn't start very well. First, you spill some cereal at breakfast and have to clean it up. Then a heavy rainstorm starts outside, so you have to find your raincoat, unjam the zipper, grab your homework, and run for a bus. But on the way, you slip on a muddy path, fall, and get the homework wet and dirty.

You get up and keep running, but you're also worrying about how to explain all this when you do get to school. Is there

· · · · · · · ·
# TALK PIDGIN, SO YOU CAN MEET A MONKEY
## *continued*

any way to make the teacher and everybody in the class understand?

**2.** Maybe there is. Check out this chart, because there are some good ways to get your own English converted into Pidgin English. See if you can put your story together.

| Pidgin English | Your English |
|---|---|
| Sori missis ticha . . . | Sorry, Teacher . . . |
| klinim bikpela mes . . . | I had to clean up a big mess . . . |
| fixim zip . . . | fix a zipper . . . |
| tumas ren . . . | there was too much rain . . . |
| fallim wantaim . . . | I fell down once . . . |
| longtaim nofindim pe em ve . . . | I had to wait for a bus . . . |
| bagarap skulmanki kago . . . | I ruined my homework . . . |

**3.** Look closely at the "Pidgin" column, and use your pencil to underline the words or parts of words that are close to your own standard English. Some are obvious, like *Teacher* and *ticha,* and you can find more by saying the Pidgin words aloud.

They sound just like they look, so *wantaim* comes out as *one time,* and *tumas* comes close to *too much.* That's why Pidgin works so well. Anybody who can say these simple words can *tok* without having to know standard English.

········
# TALK PIDGIN, SO YOU CAN MEET A MONKEY
### *continued*

**4.** For some fun, say *bikpela* a few times. Doesn't it sound like *big fellow,* and isn't that a clear way to describe a mess of spilled cereal?

*Bagarap* is a little harder. It means everything from *break* to *mess up* to *ruin,* and is almost an all-purpose word in Pidgin.

**5.** Now say the whole Pidgin column as fast as you can, from top to bottom. Repeat it a few times, and listen to yourself. You're *tokkin* Pidgin, and it makes sense.

Maybe the best part is *skulmanki.* It means *schoolmonkey,* which is what a young student is called in Papua New Guinea. So now *you're* a monkey, carrying *kago.* What would *cargo* be for a schoolmonkey? Homework?

### WORD WIZARDRY

Pidgin uses abbreviations, too. A *pe em ve* is a *PMV,* which stands for Public Motor Vehicle. Sometimes PMV *nocomin.*

········

# TALK SOME STRINE WITH YOUR MATES

· · · · · · · · · · · · · · · · · · ·

**S**uppose you fly south from Papua New Guinea, all the way down to Sydney, Australia.

Out the window, what you'll see for most of your trip is dry, reddish, empty-looking land that seems to stretch on forever. Australia is about the same size as the United States, but has a population only 7 percent as big, with half of those people living in Sydney and four other big cities.

So by the time you land, you may have the odd feeling that Australia looks like two different countries. But it certainly won't sound like two, because almost everywhere you go, you'll hear a distinct and consistent kind of English.

For a joke, some Australians call their version of English Strine instead of Australian. That's because it's often spoken oddly, with an accent that makes many words sound like vague, shortened British English.

Say *Strine* out loud a few times. Can you hear the word *Australian* in it, hiding under an accent? If you can, you might have some fun trying out Strine English, because the accent is just the beginning. Strine is also full of unique words and jokes you'll like. They come from all over "Strilya."

### Here's what you need:

*Two friends who like to try new jokes*
*Some time for the three of you to study Strine*

### Here's what you do:

1. Say two words out loud: *mate* and *might*. Then try to say something halfway between them, until you get used to the Strine way of saying *mate*. Tell your friends that you're all "mates" now, meaning that you're close friends working together.

2. Then look at the Comedy Club project on page 36.

In #4 there, you'll see that you can use three different styles to put together jokes.

What if you worked with those, but made the joke depend on Strine words? You and your friends might be able to invent something totally weird to add to the Comedy Club or try out at school.

3. Look at these Strine words, and brainstorm with your friends. There could be a way to fit them into one of your old jokes or work out a completely new one.

· · · · · · · ·
# TALK SOME STRINE WITH YOUR MATES
## *continued*

| Strine Words | Pronounced Like | Means |
|---|---|---|
| drongo | *drawn*-go | stupid person |
| G'day | gidd-*eye* | hello |
| ta | tah | thank you |
| aggro | *ag*-row | anger |
| yonks | yawnks | a lot |
| bludger | *blood*-juh | lazy person |
| dinki-di | dinki-*dee* | genuine; the real thing |
| dog and bone | dawg-'n'*bone* | telephone |
| chinwag | *chin*-wag | conversation |
| ugly as a box of blowflies | . . . *blau*-floys | extremely ugly |
| she'll be apples | . . . *epp*-ulls | everything will work out |

**4.** Once you get a basic joke, make sure that you all rehearse it enough
times to get the sound of Strine right.

When you try it with an audience, you may find that just the Strine
words will be enough to make the joke work. People always like to hear new
accents, and they'll be asking you how you came up with something so
unusual.

### WORD WIZARDRY

In Strine, almost anything can be nicknamed.

| | | |
|---|---|---|
| chalkie | = | teacher |
| oldies | = | parents |
| postie | = | mailman |
| mozzie | = | mosquito |
| lippie | = | lipstick |
| neddie | = | horse |

G'DAY, CHALKIE

# SPIN THE WORLD WORD WHEELS

The farther you go outside North America, the more places you'll find where some form of English is being spoken. The basic language has spread strongly during the past 150 years.

But you can't assume that English is now the "world language," with most people knowing enough to use it as a basic way to read, write, and talk. In fact, about five people out of six in the world use something else as their primary language. If you're a native speaker of English, you're actually in a minority.

To get a sense for what that means and what it says about you and your friends, you can try two projects between here and page 167. Both use the same materials. The first one will show you where English fits in the world right now. The second will show you how English spreads, and you can do it as an experiment with your whole class.

## Here's what you need:

*At least three paper plates, each 6 inches (15 centimeters) across*

*A calculator*

*A protractor*

*A ruler*

*Pencil and paper*

*At least two pieces of poster board, each 14 by 22 inches (35 by 55 centimeters) across*

*Three two-pronged paper fasteners*

*A set of colored markers or pens*

## Here's what you do:

1. Sit down with one paper plate and imagine that you're going to use it to represent the whole world. Also think of the plate as a compass, 360 degrees around.

2. Then look over this chart. It shows you how many people speak each of the world's five most widespread languages, with all others combined in the bottom row.

| | As Their Main Language | As a Second Language |
|---|---|---|
| Mandarin Chinese | 827 million | 930 million |
| English | 800 million | 319 million |
| Hindi | 327 million | 400 million |
| Spanish | 326 million | 371 million |
| Russian | 172 million | 291 million |
| All others | 3,548 million | 3,689 million |

# SPIN THE WORLD WORD WHEELS

## *continued*

**3.** Now do some math with your calculator. The total number of people in the world now is six *billion,* which you can also see as 6,000 million. Then look at the chart's "Main Language" column.

Enter 827 in your calculator and divide it by 6,000. You'll get 0.138, which means that 13.8 percent of all the people in the world speak Mandarin Chinese as a native language.

**4.** Write down the 13.8 percent, then divide each other number in both columns of the chart by 6,000 to get percentages. Copy your answers here or on a separate piece of paper.

|  | Percentage as Main Language | Percentage as Second Language |
|---|---|---|
| Mandarin Chinese | 13.8 | 15.5 |
| English | —— | —— |
| Hindi | —— | —— |
| Spanish | —— | —— |
| Russian | —— | —— |
| All others | —— | —— |

**5.** Now look at your plate. Remember that it's 360 degrees around, and that it also represents all six billion people in the world. You're going to turn the plate into a visual display of how many people speak each language in the "Main" column. Here's how to do that.

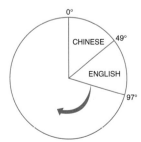

- Pencil in 0 degrees at the top of the plate.
- On the calculator, enter 360 and multiply it by 0.138. That will give you 49.7.
- Put your protractor on the plate, and mark where 49 degrees appears on the plate edge.
- Draw a section that runs from 0 to 49 degrees and label it "Chinese." Then take all the same steps with each of your numbers from the "Main" column. Draw in new sections like the "English" sample for each language.

# SPIN THE WORLD WORD WHEELS
## *continued*

**6.** Then get a second plate and repeat all these same steps using the percentages from your "Second" column. Label all sections, and use color to make them look good.

**7.** Now, so they'll work as wheels, you need to mount the two plates on your posterboard. Here's how.

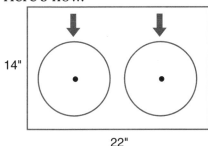

14"

22"

- With a pencil point, carefully punch holes through the centers of the plates.
- Arrange the plates on the board, then put the pencil through the centers to mark points on the board.
- Carefully use scissors to punch holes at those two points.
- Use the paper fasteners to put the plates on the board, then test them to see if they'll spin easily. If not, carefully enlarge the holes in the board.
- Color in two big arrows, as pictured.

Now you're ready. Get some friends together to spin the wheels.

Try the "Main" one first, and take turns. See where the arrow points when the plate stops spinning. It won't be "English" very often, and that will show you all just how unlikely it is for any one person out of six billion to share your first language.

Then try the "Second" wheel, to see how likely it is that you could travel the world and find people who could easily understand. The more turns both plates need to find you, the more unusual you and your language really are.

### WORD WIZARDRY

Say hello to your Mom.

|            |       |
|------------|-------|
| In Latin:   | Mater |
| In Spanish: | Madre |
| In German:  | Mutti |
| In Russian: | Mat   |

## SPIN WORD WHEELS FOR YOUR CLASS

**L**ook at the back of a U.S. dollar bill. "*E pluribus unum*," it says in Latin, meaning that one country (*unum*) has been built by people from many places (*E pluribus*).

To see why that's not just true, but important, think about your own family. Were you or your parents born in some other country? What language did your parents grow up speaking? If it was English, what about your grandparents? Or your great-grandparents?

Now think about your whole class. You could see it as a sort of small *unum,* with everyone in it part of the *pluribus.* Their families came from somewhere else, too, just like yours. And if you could organize a way to find out the details, what everybody could see is how and why the class happened to become a *unum.*

All you need to do is make a few changes in the "World Word Wheels" you built on page 161.

. . . . . . . .

# SPIN WORD WHEELS FOR YOUR CLASS
## *continued*

### *Here's what you need:*

*All the same materials listed on page 161, plus:*
    *Graph paper*
    *Permission to use a copying machine*

### *Here's what you do:*

**1.** Use one piece of graph paper to draw a large, neat chart like this one.

**Which Languages Did These People Grow Up Speaking?**

| Student | Both Parents | Any Two Grandparents | Any Two Great-Grandparents |
|---|---|---|---|
| | | | |
| | | | |
| | | | |
| | | | |

Then go to the machine and make one copy for each person in the class.

**2.** Ask your classmates to get help from a parent to fill in their charts as completely as possible. Give them a few days to get it done, then collect all the charts and check them over. What you need to find is exactly how many times "English" appears in the boxes, and in which columns. Do the same for all the other languages, then use a blank piece of graph paper to lay out the answers. Here's an example of how that might look.

· · · · · · · ·

# SPIN WORD WHEELS FOR YOUR CLASS
## *continued*

### *Sample* Chart

| Language | Students | Parents | Grandparents | Great-Grandparents |
|----------|----------|---------|--------------|--------------------|
| English | 16 | 28 | 48 | 68 |
| Spanish | 2 | 6 | 11 | 19 |
| Chinese | 1 | 3 | 5 | 12 |
| ? | 1 | 4 | 10 | 34 |
| ? | | 3 | 7 | 24 |
| ? | | | 7 | 19 |

3. If you want, you can then make a big, poster-size version of the answers to show in class. Everybody will see the pattern for
   • how languages change when families move from country to country,
   • how long the changes have taken for the families in your class, and
   • how English has become the main language for your class.

4. To go one step further, you can also use wheels to show how languages in your class compare with those in the whole United States. Make two wheels, just the way you did on page 163.

   Call the first wheel "United States," and use these numbers to draw the lines on it and to label the sections.

| Label for Section | Degrees to Draw |
|-------------------|-----------------|
| English | 0 to 320 |
| Spanish | 320 to 325 |
| French or German | 325 to 327 |
| All others | 327 to 360 |

. . . . . . . .
# SPIN WORD WHEELS FOR YOUR CLASS
## *continued*

Call the second wheel "Class," and use your real numbers to divide the wheel into sections. For example, if there are 20 students in your class and 16 have grown up speaking English, use 80 percent of the wheel (0 to 288 degrees) for the "English" section. If 2 of the 20 grew up with Spanish, make that section 10 percent of the wheel (288 to 324 degrees), and keep going until you've used up the full, 360-degree wheel.

5. Once both wheels are made and mounted on the poster board, you can have everybody step up and take turns spinning. Each student will see how likely it is to be "typical" in both the whole class and the whole country.

At the end, you and your classmates will have clear ideas of how family backgrounds change as the years go by. You'll also see how one main language like English slowly takes over in a country as people move there from other places.

### WORD WIZARDRY

Five U.S. states have large numbers of people who speak something other than English as a first *or* second language.

| | |
|---|---|
| California | 31 percent |
| Texas | 25 percent |
| New York | 23 percent |
| New Jersey | 19 percent |
| Florida | 17 percent |

.......
# MAKE THE WEB REALLY WORLDWIDE
. . . . . . . . . . . . . . . . . . . .

**I**f you like looking around on the Internet, you know that the only real limit to it is your own curiosity. You can play new games, send E-mail, check through encyclopedias, read books, and even tour art museums thousands of miles away.

You can also use it to get an idea of what's really going on in other countries every day. Like most big newspapers in North America, many Asian and European papers run their own sites and update them every few hours.

Maybe you'd like to check out a few. You'll see some big differences in what's considered to be news, and also some small differences in how English gets used around the world.

### Here's what you need:

*A connection to the Internet at school or at home*
*Fifteen minutes to tour some sites*

### Here's what you do:

1. Decide which one of the countries listed here interests you most, then go to the World Wide Web (WWW) site shown for one of the newspapers there. Maybe you'd like to try New Zealand first, because it's already tomorrow there. How many chances do you ever get to read tomorrow's paper?

| Country | Newspaper | Site Name |
|---|---|---|
| New Zealand | *Wairarapa Times-Age* | http://times-age.co.nz/daily |
| India | *Hindustan Times* | www.hindustantimes.com |
| China | *Hong Kong Standard* | www.hkstandard.com |
| Shetland Islands | *Shetland Times* | www.shetland-times.co.uk |
| Kenya | *Daily Nation* | www.nationaudio.com/News/ |

*Note: In 1999, all of these sites were free, and allowed you to look through several pages in each day's edition.*

. . . . . . . .

# MAKE THE WEB REALLY WORLDWIDE
## *continued*

**2.** When you check the papers, notice how much British English is used around the world. Look for British ways of writing and spelling, like these:

| **British English** | **American English** |
| --- | --- |
| He played *football whilst at* school | He played *soccer while in* school |
| United States *Win* Davis Cup | United States *Wins* Davis Cup |
| *Juggernaut Crash* on *Motorway* | *Semitrailer Wreck* on *Freeway* |
| She *paid in* a *checque* at the bank | She *deposited* a *check* at the bank |
| *Holidaymakers Throng Seaside* | *Vacationers Crowd Beaches* |

Keep an eye out for the thousands of small differences between the British and American versions of English. You'll enjoy finding them, partly because most of them won't really confuse you.

**3.** If what you see on the newspaper sites is interesting, "bookmark" them so you can come back on other days to check what's going on. Most connections to the Internet allow you to do that by holding down your Control key (Ctrl) and typing "D" on the keyboard.

**4.** Then work on extending your tour with these two sites. They'll take you all around Asia, and then all the way off Planet Earth. Check them out.

http://www.askasia.org/adult_free_zone/afz.htm

http://jpl.nasa.gov

### WORD WIZARDRY

Look at this, too:

http://sln.fi.edu/tfi/hotlists/kids.html.

The whole site was designed by kids. You can see what they're doing for new hobbies and projects, and maybe send in something of your own.

# CAPTURE A COUNTRY (WITH ART)

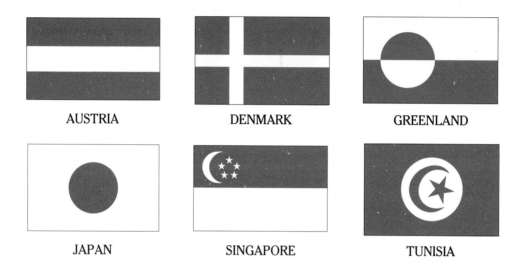

AUSTRIA          DENMARK          GREENLAND

JAPAN          SINGAPORE          TUNISIA

**D**uring the last 50 years, more and more brands, teams, and businesses have started to use logos as signatures. They believe that strong, simple designs can work like a name, and also that the right design can suggest something special behind the name.

For countries, flags have always served that purpose. Flag colors and designs symbolize "who" a country is, especially for the people who live there.

To see how simple colors and shapes can do something so important, here's an experiment you can try.

# CAPTURE A COUNTRY (WITH ART)
## *continued*

### *Here's what you need:*

*Books and other information about a country that interests you*

*Plenty of paper*

*A set of colored pencils, pens, or markers*

history     animals
colors     oceans
alphabets     mountains
inventions     music
famous people     religions
trees     cities

### *Here's what you do:*

1. Look at the flag for the country you like. Then suppose that you want to design something new. It won't be a new flag for the country, but a logo. How can you do that?

2. Check through the books and other information you have about the country. You need to find things that *look* so unique that they could come only from that country. Think about:

3. If you think widely enough, you'll probably come up with one or two beginning ideas to sketch. Try them out in several colors and shapes, to see if you can make them get simpler and clearer as you work. Good logos need to be strong, but not complicated.

4. Do a final, careful version of your favorite in color.

When you're done, think about showing your finished work to parents or friends. Tell them that it's a logo for a country, and ask if they can name the country. Then ask them to describe the country's flag. What you may find is that not many people really know the flags of foreign countries.

### WORD WIZARDRY

People always say that "a picture is worth a thousand words." How many words is a logo worth? Could a word be worth a thousand pictures?

# GIVE THE WORLD A GLYPH

No matter where you go in the world, you'll see dozens of signs like these. They're called glyphs, and pronounced *gliffs*.

There are so many of them because they do such a good job of communicating ideas without using words. A traveler going from Germany to France to England doesn't have to know what "rauchen verboten," "defense de fumer," and "smoking prohibited" all mean. He just sees the glyph.

New glyphs are being invented all the time to make communication easier around the world. If you like art, maybe there's an opportunity here for you.

········
# GIVE THE WORLD A GLYPH
## *continued*

### *Here's what you need:*

*Paper*
*A set of colored pencils or markers*

### *Here's what you do:*

1. Think about practical signs the whole world could use every day. How can you draw symbols so clear and simple that anybody anywhere would understand?

   Start your thinking with these five ideas. More will probably occur to you as you work.

   - This water is safe to drink.
   - No noise of any kind is allowed here.
   - This road has deep holes in it.
   - Everyone is welcome here.
   - You have arrived too late.

2. While you sketch possibilities, think about color and shape. If you've designed signs or logos for other projects, you know that even basic shapes "say" something.

3. Once you have one or two good sketches, see how much simpler you can make them. The best glyphs can't be too complicated. They need to work instantly, for everybody.

4. Finish and color versions of your best ideas.

When you're done, test out your glyphs with a few of your friends. If they all understand right away and if they all see exactly the same message, maybe you're onto something.

### WORD WIZARDRY

Imagine a student in your class, and also an elderly monk walking down a road in Thailand. What are the two things that both people would understand immediately? A number and a glyph?

# 9. COMMUNICATE WITH COMPUTERS

**M**aybe you already do your homework on a computer, surf the Internet, send E-mail, and play computer games.

But whatever you're doing now with computers, you'll probably be doing a little more next month, then a lot more next year. Computers just pull you along, constantly showing you new ways to pick up ideas, poke into them, and create your own.

Even now, there's almost no limit to the ideas you can get to with a computer. Do you want to see a poster for the movie that's number one in Kuala Lumpur this week? Or find out who kicked how many field goals for the Philadelphia Eagles in 1991? To see how, look at page 181.

But remember that computers are for *your* ideas, too. You can write and draw with them, and move words, pictures, and paragraphs around on the screen. You can send messages and set up games, do your homework, or design a home page that's all your own.

All you need is a little time on a computer at school or at home, plus some imagination. Give it a try.

. . . . . . . .
# WRITE A STORY ON THE SNEAKERNET
. . . . . . . . . . . . . . . . . . . .

**B**efore the Internet and before E-mail, Sneakernet was how ideas got from one computer to another. All you needed was a diskette for the idea and sneakers for your feet.

Sneakernet wasn't too elegant, but it worked, and it still does. In fact, it's a particularly good way for a group of friends to work together.

Think about it. What's the simplest, easiest way for four or five friends to use computers to cooperate on writing a story?

Probably Sneakernet, because it gives you a way to take turns, and also because you can use one computer or more than one. Here's all you need to do.

First, remember that the story is more important than the computer. Think up some rules for the story original enough to guarantee that your friends will be interested in trying it. Maybe a set of rules like these could work:

- The story has to be exactly 20 sentences long, with each friend writing an equal share.
- Absolutely anything can happen in the story.
- The ending of the story has to be both happy and sad.

· · · · · · · ·
# WRITE A STORY ON THE SNEAKERNET
## *continued*

Use a PC at school or at home to write your share of the story first. When you're done writing, click on "save" to make sure that your work isn't lost. Then put a diskette into the PC's floppy drive and click on "copy." Type in **a:** if the PC asks you for the "destination" of the copy you're making.

That will put your share of the story onto the diskette. Push the button to get it out of the floppy drive, then lace up your sneakers and take it to the next writer. All that friend has to do is put it in a floppy drive, click **a:**, and click "open" to see the story's beginning and start adding to it. Then it's "save," "copy," and **a:** again, and the diskette goes to the next person in the group.

When you're all done, get together to read the story. Except for the last writer, each of you knows only parts of the story, and it'll be fun for everybody to see how the plot developed.

### WORD WIZARDRY

Look at "Do English a Favor" on page 222. If you say "copy" to a PC, why does it say "destination"? Why couldn't it say "copy onto what?"

## POINT AND CLICK SOME PLAIN ENGLISH

**I**f you use the Internet regularly, you've probably run across a number of sites that show you excellent graphics but not very good English. They hit you with "Limk hear," "Entery point," or ">>>subsequent Warrior>," all surrounded by big visual effects.

Worse, you're often forced to guess your way through instructions that seem written to *hide* what you should do next, such as "Select [\] closure for New Battle."

It's frustrating, because bad English can make you give up on a site with games or links that at first looked promising.

But if you have E-mail, maybe there's something you can do.

### Here's what you need:

*An Internet account that lets you send E-mail free*

*Permission from a parent or teacher to use E-mail*

*A pencil*

*A piece of scrap paper*

### Here's what you do:

**1.** The next time you log on, make sure you have the pencil and paper handy. What you're looking for are sites where everything but the writing has been done well.

**2.** If you already know one or two such sites, go there directly and take notes. Write down the E-mail addresses for those sites, and carefully copy the piece of writing that you think is badly done or unnecessarily confusing.

**3.** If you don't have particular sites in mind, just keep an eye out for bad English as you go. You *will* find some, and when you do, be sure to copy down both the E-mail address for each site and the writing problems you find.

**4.** Once you have your notes, log off. Then spend time translating the bad writing you found into good, correct English. Make the meaning as plain and clear as you can.

········
# POINT AND CLICK SOME PLAIN ENGLISH
## *continued*

That will get you ready for the next time you're on the Net, when you can send an E-mail suggesting your improvements. Think about sending a message like the sample below. Because it's designed to go to more than one site, you may find that you'll get some action. Webmasters want to be on lists that rank as "cool sites," not "bad writing" ones.

### *Dear [site names],*

Many of us in my grade really like the way your sites look. But we wonder about the spelling and writing mistakes on your main pages. We also find that it's so confusing to get from one page to another.

For a start, here are some errors that would be easy to fix:

1. Spelling:
   [For each site, quote the mistake exactly as you found it, and name the page where it appears. Then supply the correct spelling.]
2. Unclear links or instructions:
   [For each site, quote the unclear language, and name the page where you found it. Then type in your improved version.]

We'll be interested to see what you do. The writing ought to be as good as the art, don't you think?

Sincerely,
[your screen name]

### WORD WIZARDRY

Fifteen years ago, the Internet could carry words, numbers, and links to only a few hundred "official" sites. Now everybody can use it, and there may not even be a way to count the millions of links being used at any one time.

. . . . . . . .
# SEND A FRIEND A COMPUTER ROSE
. . . . . . . . . . . . . . . . . . .

**P**eople often think of a computer as just a machine. But when you use one to write a letter or send E-mail, you can play with some of the keys to show that you're happy, amused, angry, or surprised. You can cartoon a few funny faces or even send an electronic rose, just with the keys.

### Here's what you need:

*Permission to try some experiments with a computer keyboard*

*Someone to help, if you haven't used a computer much*

### Here's what you do:

1. Create a smiley face that might look good with a joke or with your name. To make the face, type in a colon and then a right-hand parenthesis mark. You'll get:

## : )

*Hint: To make the face show up well, put it in bold type and use a larger type size.*

2. Make a big, sideways smile. Key in a colon and then a capital D. You'll get:

## :D

3. Wink at your reader. Type in a semicolon, then a hyphen for a nose, and then a right-hand parenthesis mark. You'll get:

## ;-)

4. Make a sideways surprised face. Key in a colon and then a capital O, to get:

## :O

5. Try out some fancier faces. Look around on the keyboard for slashes, dashes, semicolons, and colons, so that you can type in some hair or a big nose.

6. Now design a computer rose for someone special. Here's how.

   • Key in @, the symbol for "at." It's on the key for the number 2, and you get it by holding down the "Shift" key while you type 2.

   (You're using @ to draw a rosebud, but people mostly use it to write about prices or locations. For instance, maybe you could buy a dozen roses @ $1 each.)

   • Now key in two hyphens (--) to start the stem for your rose.

   • Next, key in a leaf by using an arrow sign (>). You get that by holding down "Shift" while you use the key for period.

· · · · · · · ·

# SEND A FRIEND A COMPUTER ROSE

## *continued*

- Finish the stem with several more hyphens, and you'll have:

Do that in reverse order, and you get:

Maybe you'll want to send a dozen roses to someone really special.

### WORD WIZARDRY

If you use Windows, open up Word and click "Insert." Then click "Symbol" on the menu that appears. You'll start seeing whole sets of shapes you can use for drawing, such as ≋, ⌇, ∅, and ✿.

# BUILD YOUR BOOKMARK LIST

**P**robably the best thing about using the Internet is that you can find out about anything you want, anytime you want.

But that can be a problem, too. There's so much information available that clicking your way through it can get confusing or distracting, and sometimes both. Once you've looked at enough sites during any one session, you can even forget why you logged on in the first place.

The best ways to organize your time on the Internet are to use search engines and bookmarks. *Search engines* might be an odd term, but what they do is so useful that once you learn, you'll probably use them over and over.

### *Here's how to get started:*

1. Log onto this site: **http://sunsite.berkeley.edu/InternetIndex**.
2. Click on **Kids**, then on **Kids' Tools for Searching the Internet**.
3. You'll see a set of boxes, all labeled with names like "StudyWEB," "Kids Click!," and "Yahooligans!" Click inside one of the boxes.
4. Behind all these boxes are search engines, which will start running for you as soon as you type a subject into a box. For example, depending on how much you want to know, you could type in:

> **earthquakes** or
> **earthquakes** + **Japan** or
> **earthquakes** + **Japan** + **predictions**

The more key words you give a search engine, the more exact its search will be for sites that have the information you want. After you key in your words and click on **Search**, you'll see a full list of those sites pop onto the screen. You can then click on the ones that look best.

When you're through with a site, go to the top of your screen and click on **Back**. That will return you to the list, so you can try other sites.

5. When you do find a site you like, think about "bookmarking" it, so that you can come back to it whenever you want without having to do another search. To bookmark a site once you're in it, hold

· · · · · · · ·
# BUILD YOUR BOOKMARK LIST
## *continued*

down the **Ctrl** key and type **D**. That tells the network to list the site under your account, so that it will automatically be there on a list the next time you log on.

6. Doing bookmarks saves you time and also lets you start building your own personal Internet library. All your bookmarks show up on a list, and returning to a site just takes a click on its name.

The more you customize the Internet, the better and faster it will work for you.

### WORD WIZARDRY

| If You Like | Go To |
|---|---|
| Astronomy | http://antwrp.gsfc.nasa.gov/apod/ astropix.html |
| Football | http://www.nfl.com/ |
| Math | http://www.ee.surrey.uk/Personal/R.Knott/ Fib/fibnet.html |
| Computer games | http://www.freegaming.nu/ |
| Animal photos | http://www.si.edu/organize/museums/zoo/ photos/phoset.htm |

# GET YOUR START AS A WEBMASTER

**H**ave you ever thought about building your own home page on the Internet? Or maybe a page for your whole class?

It's not so hard, and many of the networks that run in schools will even help you do it. All you need to do first is check with a parent or teacher, to make sure that your network will allow you to have a home page without charging for it. If there's no charge, and if your parent(s) or teacher approves, you can get started as soon as you have an hour available.

### Here's what you need:

*The OK to do this, on a network that allows its customers to build personal home pages*

*A supply of sketch paper, and about an hour to plan what will be on your page*

*Another hour, maybe with a friend or teacher, to get your page onto the network*

### Here's what you do:

1. Remember all the sites you've already seen. You liked some much better than others. Think about what *basic* designs and *basic* information made them seem interesting. At first, don't think about the fancy art, colors, frames, buttons, and pop-ups that are on so many sites. Your own page doesn't have to be fancy when you get it started, but it does have to be interesting if you want other people to look at it.

2. Start by asking yourself questions like these:
   * What's my page about? Just me, and what I like? Or is it also about my friends, my family, my class, or my team?
   * Why would anyone be interested in my page? What can I show that other people would probably care about?
   * Am I just having fun with the page, or do I want people to think about what I show?

3. Once you're clear on why you're creating the page, try sketching out a few designs. It's not much different from making a poster or designing the front page of a newsletter. You need to use the page area so that your best art and words are emphasized, with all your other ideas arranged to support them. There's no one "right" way to design a page, but here's a basic idea that you can probably improve.

· · · · · · · ·
# GET YOUR START AS A WEBMASTER
## *continued*

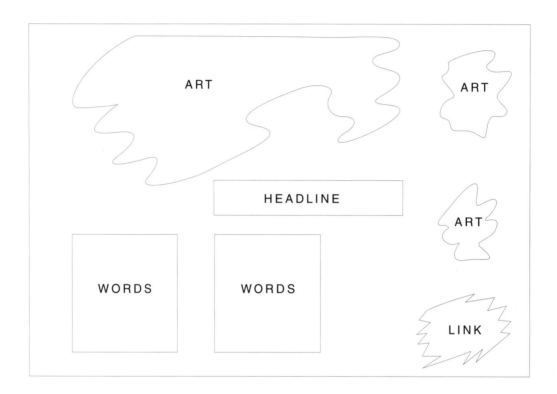

**4.** If you want additional ideas, look at these sites the next time you're on the Internet. They were all designed by students during the past few years and use everything from a running panther to a recording of the school song.

| School | Home Page |
|---|---|
| Kamogawa School<br>Kamogawa City, Japan | http://www.ki-net.co.jp/~kamosho/eindex.html |
| Mountain Grove Middle School<br>Mountain Grove, Missouri | http://204.184.227.130/ms/ |
| Thomas Jefferson Middle School<br>Edison, New Jersey | http://www.garden.net/users/thomasj/ |

· · · · · · · ·

# GET YOUR START AS A WEBMASTER

## *continued*

5. When you're satisfied with your own personal design, log onto your network and ask your friend or teacher to do some work with you.

    Basically, what you need to do is turn your home-page sketch into an electronic version that will be accepted and kept by the network, so that you and other people can find it. To get that done, you may initially need some help finding the part of your network that accepts new home pages.

    But when you do, you'll probably also find a set of directions and a blank home page right on your screen.

6. Then the job is to type in your own page's words, work with typefaces, and move words around to match your design. That's the fun part, and so is using any art software that's available on the network or at school. With the right software and a scanner, you can even send your own drawings or photos right to the home page.

    But keep looking back at #2 above, so that you have a good reason for using the art.

7. Be sure to add an E-mail address at the end of your page.

### WORD WIZARDRY

The Internet can send your ideas anywhere in the world, instantly. Make them good.

# 10. SOLVE ALPHABET MYSTERIES

1. B-U-S

2.

3. バス

**M**aybe there's not much mystery about the word *bus* and a picture of a bus, but what about the Japanese symbol?

It means "bus," too. It's written in modern Japanese, just one of the mysterious alphabet systems you may want to try.

Would you like to create an ancient Egyptian hieroglyphic, or learn the Navy's alphabet flag signals? Would you like to design highly useful word pictures, or use sign language to make a name for yourself? How about finding a lost letter of the alphabet, possibly the next time you go past an antiques store?

You can try alphabets from around the world and look at strange ways of writing, including an ancient writing mystery that no one can solve. Maybe you'd like to see a system of writing that almost saved an Indian nation.

You can even bake an alphabet that's good to eat.

# Try Out Alphabets Around the World

If you like calligraphy, you'll like trying out your skills on alphabets from around the world. At first, the strange letters may seem completely mysterious to you. Yet millions of people read from them every day.

Here's a way to practice Arabic and Hebrew scripts that Moslem and Jewish students learn as part of their religions. Then you can try out the historic Greek and German alphabets, and practice your penmanship skills by trying Cherokee writing.

You can even write in an alphabet designed by saints. More than a thousand years ago, two Greek brothers, Cyril and Methodius, designed a new alphabet as part of their mission to convert the people of Moravia to Christianity. They taught people so well that they were both elevated to sainthood, and their alphabet found its way across the Slavic and Russian lands. That alphabet is now called the Cyrillic alphabet, named for Saint Cyril himself.

***Here are six beautiful letters to try, just to give you an idea:***

**1.** A letter from the Arabic alphabet character (the dad, a *th* sound)

**2.** A letter from the Cherokee alphabet (the *yu* sound)

**3.** A letter from the Cyrillic alphabet (the *zh* sound)

**4.** A letter in German script (the z or *tset* sound)

· · · · · · · ·

# TRY OUT ALPHABETS AROUND THE WORLD
## *continued*

**5.** A letter from the Greek alphabet (the delta, a *d* sound)

**6.** A letter from the Hebrew alphabet (the aleph, the *a* sound, although usually silent)

### WORD WIZARDRY

What maker of alphabets has a tree named after him? The sequoia (Sequoyah) redwood is the largest and tallest living thing on earth, so it must be named after an especially great person. Sequoyah of the Cherokee nation was that person. For 12 years, he worked hard on a writing system for the Cherokee language. Each of Sequoyah's 85 symbols stands for a syllable, and together they represent every sound in the Cherokee language.

His system of writing was partly an alphabet and partly a syllabary. That's a way of writing symbols for each syllable rather than each sound in a language.

Sequoyah established the first Cherokee newspapers and books. For a short period, the Cherokee people were able to live as a separate nation, with the first public school system in America. Despite the many tragedies and disasters that followed them in later years and destroyed them as a separate nation, the Cherokee people always kept their love of learning, reading, and writing. Most Cherokees speak English now and are citizens of the United States. But whenever we see a great tree, we can remember a great Cherokee leader.

. . . . . . . .
# DESIGN YOUR OWN WORD PICTURES

. . . . . . . . . . . . . . . . . . . .

The first writers had no alphabet. Instead, they drew a picture or symbol for each word, something that people could understand easily, such as a circle for a sun or stick figures for human beings.

Now we have letters of the alphabet that stand for vowel and consonant sounds. But we still have a few useful symbols that stand for whole words. They're called logograms.

Look at the top of a keyboard, for instance, and you'll probably see a whole row of logograms.

Here are a few logograms and their meanings. See if you can make a match:

| | |
|---|---|
| $ | percent |
| # | equals |
| % | divided by |
| & | copyright |
| = | and |
| ÷ | pound |
| © | dollar |

(Look for the matches on page 205.)

Now see if you can create a useful logogram of your own. Maybe you can create one that is so useful that other people will want to use it, too.

### Create a symbol to describe a few of these words:

1. On

2. Off

3. Increasing volume, louder

4. Decreasing volume, quieter

5. For sale

6. Rising temperatures, warmer

7. Lower temperatures, colder

8. High nutritional value

9. Low nutritional value

10. Strong

11. Weak

········

# DESIGN YOUR OWN WORD PICTURES
## *continued*

### WORD WIZARDRY

The first writing was nearly all logograms. If you wanted to write about an ox (or a boy or a horse), you drew a picture. Then, if you got used to drawing many pictures of a boy or a horse, you started to make then simpler. People still knew what you meant. Eventually, the pictures came to stand for consonants or vowels instead of whole words, and maybe they took a tilt or a turnaround and ended up as one of the letters of our alphabet. Just look at how a logogram for ox became our letter A:

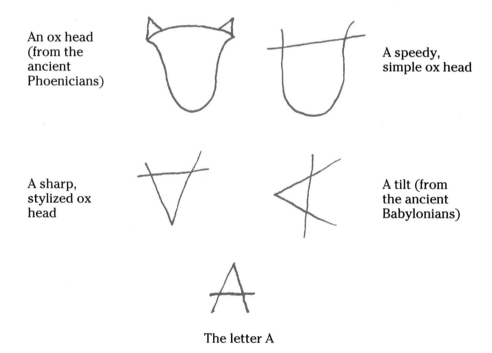

An ox head (from the ancient Phoenicians)

A speedy, simple ox head

A sharp, stylized ox head

A tilt (from the ancient Babylonians)

The letter A

# CREATE YOUR OWN HIEROGLYPHICS

**I**f you knew how to write well in ancient Egypt, you could become a scribe, one of the most powerful people around. The pharaoh might ask you for help with writing. You might even rise to become pharaoh yourself.

Of course, it was not that easy to learn to write well back then. You would need to learn a basic 27 signs that represented sounds. Then you would want to memorize at least 700 more to mean words, ideas, and syllables. These signs often looked more like complex drawings than simple letters.

They were the famous Egyptian hieroglyphics. Here's how you can make a hieroglyphic stone that looks almost as if you had Egyptian ancestors who handed it down to you. It is not really stone—it's plaster of paris, with your own artistic touch.

## Here's what you need:

*A reference book that pictures the basic Egyptian hieroglyphics that match best to modern sounds*

*Scrap paper and a pencil*

*A disposable pan, such as a foil or light plastic pan that you might get with take-out or delicatessen food, in a size and shape you like*

*Plaster of paris*

*Water*

*A paper towel*

*Shortening*

*A putty knife*

*A pointed knife or a wooden stick, such as a chopstick or barbecue skewer*

*Old newspapers, if you wish*

*Scissors or a craft knife*

*Acrylic paints and brushes*

*Steel wool, if you wish*

## Here's what you do:

**1.** Decide what hieroglyphics you want to write onto your stone. Perhaps you want to spell a name. You may wish to add artwork in the Egyptian style. Practice your design with scrap paper and pencil first. Write your hieroglyphics from top to bottom.

········
# CREATE YOUR OWN HIEROGLYPHICS
*continued*

2. Choose a foil or plastic pan in a size and shape you like for your artwork. With a paper towel, rub shortening over the pan.

3. Mix plaster of paris with water according to directions on the bag. Depending on the size of your pan, you'll need about 6 cups (1.5 liters) plaster of paris mixed with about 4 cups (about 1 liter) water.

4. Fill the pan with the plaster-of-paris mixture. Use a putty knife to level off the surface so that the plaster is even with the edges of the pan.

5. Use a pointed knife or wooden stick to carve in your hiero-glyphics and other artwork.

6. Set the mold to dry for at least 24 hours.

7. Remove your hieroglyphic stone from the pan. Put down old newspapers, if you wish, and use scissors or a craft knife to help cut away the pan. Use the knife or stick to get rid of rough edges or bubbles.

> *Caution: You may need an adult to help you with the craft knife.*

8. Use acrylic paints and brushes to paint your artwork. To make it look as if it came straight from ancient Egypt, use natural, earthy tones of green, blue, black, yellow, red, and white.

9. If you want your work to look as if it's been around several thousand years, you may want to use steel wool to rub away a few spots here and there. Display your work with pride. You're following in the greatest of footsteps.

## WORD WIZARDRY

Over time, the ancient Egyptians developed a second, simpler way of writing, a sort of shorthand for ordinary people. They retained a more complex system for priests and scholars. Some modern systems of writing have two (or more) levels of complexity. For example, you could take years to learn the ten thousand characters of traditional Chinese script. Yet ordinary people need to be able to read and write. And in modern times, people want to use key-boards, and a keyboard with thousands of characters would be too big and complex for any regular computer. So the Chinese solve the problem with software.

· · · · · · · ·
# WRITE UP AND DOWN AND ALL AROUND
· · · · · · · · · · · · · · · · · · · ·

**W**e write sentences across a line, from left to right. But not all people write like that. Some write right to left. Some write up to down. A few write down to up.

The ancient Greeks wrote in two directions, left to right, then right to left on the next line. The name for this system was *boustophedon,* or "ox turning." The comparison was to an ox plowing a field by going back and forth, in first one direction and then another. The Greeks also used all capital letters, with no spaces between the words and no punctuation.

THATWOULDBE

DAEROTDRAH

WOULDNTIT?

Here's a way to write a one-of-a-kind greeting. This writing direction is so unusual that you must be sure to use it only for very special occasions. It's an elegant spiral.

### Here's what you need:

*Scrap or graph paper and a pencil*

*Card paper, construction paper, poster board, or other thick paper*

*A drawing compass*

*Coloring pens, markers, or pencils*

### Here's what you do:

**1.** Practice with pencil on scrap or graph paper first, until you get the effect you want.

**2.** Make a point with your drawing compass. Use it to draw three half-circles, each about $1/2$ inch (1 graph square or 1 or 2 centimeters) wider than the next.

· · · · · · · ·
# WRITE UP AND DOWN AND ALL AROUND
## *continued*

**3.** Now use your drawing compass to mark a second point, about $1/2$ inch (1 graph square or 1 or 2 centimeters) from the first. From that point, draw three more half-circles on the other side, each about $1/2$ inch (1 graph square or 1 or 2 centimeters) wider than the next.

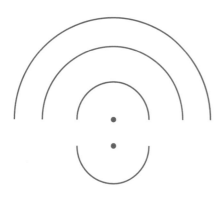

**4.** Connect the circles into a spiral. Write a greeting or an alphabet all around the spiral. Write

on the outside of the circles. If you wish, erase the circle guidelines.

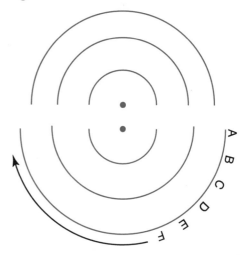

**5.** When you are happy with the results, transfer your work to good paper, such as card paper, construction paper, or poster board. Fill in with coloring pens, markers, or pencils.

Now you have an elaborate greeting for a special occasion. If you're ambitious, you can try this with even more half-circles and a larger spiral.

. . . . . . . .

# WRITE UP AND DOWN AND ALL AROUND
## *continued*

### WORD WIZARDRY

Here's an alphabet mystery. The people of Easter Island in the South Pacific wrote on wooden tablets, and their writing was really hard to read. First, they wrote left to right. Then the next line would be left to right, upside down. Then they'd write a line left to right again. Then it would be right to left, upside down. This is called Rongo-Rongo writing, and no one has ever seen anything like it. Even though some of the writing is fairly recent, just over a hundred years old, no one has any idea what the writing means. Will anyone ever figure out the mystery of Rongo-Rongo?

. . . . . . . .

# PUZZLE WITH THE ALPHABET

. . . . . . . . . . . . . . . . . . . .

**H**ere's a quick alphabet puzzle.

Write a sentence using all 26 letters of the alphabet. The challenge is to make your sentence as short as possible. Your sentence can be sensible or silly; most such sentences end up very silly.

### *Here are some funny examples:*

- The quick brown fox jumps over the lazy dog.
- The wizard jumped quickly over seven gray boxes.
- Pack my box with five dozen lacquer jugs.

### WORD WIZARDRY

Sentences like these are called pangrams. People make them up as a game—and then use them to practice typing all the letters on a keyboard or to practice calligraphy. Another name for alphabet sentences is abcedarium.

# PLAY A GAME WITH THE ALPHABET, AND C-D-C BESIDES

**H**ave you ever noticed that letters of the alphabet sometimes sound like whole words? Perhaps you've seen the letter *U* used to mean "you," or *Y* to mean "why." This game uses letters of the alphabet to make up funny phrases, silly sentences, and maybe even a whole conversation. So, if you think silly, C-D-C can mean "See the Sea."

These are like tongue twisters or pangrams: the sillier the better.

*Here are just a few rules to make the game more fun:*

1. Do not pronounce your words carefully. For example, pronounce *D* as "dee" and you have a sloppy way to pronounce *the*. Pronounce *V* as "vee" and you can use it to mean *we*. Or *N* can mean *and*.

2. You can combine the alphabet words with real words.

3. You can put together two letters of the alphabet to make a plural. For example, *EE* could mean "E's"—or "ease." *EE-Z* could mean "E's plus Z"—or "easy."

*See if you can figure out these, before you go on to make up your own:*

## One

### A Silly Seashore Verse

A sailor went to C C C
To see what he could C C C.
But all that he could C C C
Was the bottom of the
great blue C C C.

## Two

### A Conversation at a Restaurant

F U N E X?
O S, V F X.
F U N E M?
O S, V F M.
OK, L F M N X.

## Three

### A Slogan for Word Wizards

XL with EE

## Four

### What Happens When You're a Word Wizard

U R Y Y

(If you need help to figure these out, look on page 205.)

# MAKE A NAME FOR YOURSELF IN SIGN LANGUAGE

W hat's the fourth most commonly used language in the United States? It's American Sign Language, sometimes called Ameslan.

Like any other language, American Sign Language has a set of rules for grammar and word usage. It's just as complicated as any other language, and people can communicate just as well as they can in any other language. Almost every country of the world has its own unique sign language, almost as many as there are spoken languages.

What's different is that people use their hands for this language.

But imagine going through each letter of the alphabet every time you wanted to sign a message. You'd be worn out. People who use sign language have signs for each letter of the alphabet, but they also have signs for many words. And they can put signs together to form new words, especially a special name for themselves. You can design a special sign for your own name, and then perhaps you can use it to talk to someone you like.

When you get a chance, get someone to show you the shapes and movements of the signs. You can see them better in real life than you can from pictures. You'll find that often you can figure out the signs before anyone tells you the meaning. They make sense.

### Here's how to create a name for yourself in sign language:

1. Find the sign for the first letter of your name. That's the first sign for your sign-language name.

2. Then think about something you especially like, or a word that describes you well. Find the sign for that word. Perhaps you would like to show that you like bicycles, baseball, art, or photography. Perhaps you're a funny or loving person.

3. Now put the two signs together and sign a special name for yourself. Of course, you should make sure your friends also know your whole name. Many people with a hearing impairment like to speak or write words, as well as signing them—especially when those are words as important as the name of a friend.

# MAKE A NAME FOR YOURSELF IN SIGN LANGUAGE

## *continued*

John, who likes bicycles

Ann, who likes ice skating

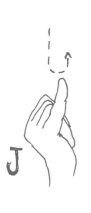

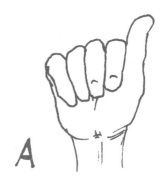

**BICYCLE**
Move fists forward in alternate circles.

**ICE SKATING**
With fingers forming the letter *X*, move the hands alternately forward and backward.

Mary, who is an artist

Daniel, who likes baseball

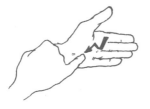

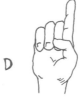

**ART, DRAW**
Trace a wavy line over the left palm with the right pinky.

**BASEBALL**
Place the right fist above the left and swing them forward as if swinging a bat.

· · · · · · · ·

# MAKE A NAME FOR YOURSELF IN SIGN LANGUAGE

## *continued*

Suzanne, who is a loving person

Fred, your neighbor

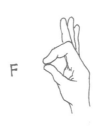 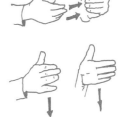

**I LOVE YOU**
Hold up the right hand with the palm facing forward and the thumb, index finger, and pinky extended.

**NEIGHBOR**
Hold the left curved hand away from the body, with the palm facing in. Move the back of the right curved hand close to the palm of the left. Then bring both flat hands down with the palms facing each other.

### WORD WIZARDRY

American Sign Language has unique grammar and word order, different from English. But most people with a hearing impairment know how to communicate in the languages of hearing people. So they can understand sign language that uses English word order.

Almost all hearing-impaired people have family who can hear. Did you know that more than 90 percent of hearing-impaired children are born to hearing parents?

Thomas Gallaudet is the man who established education for the deaf in America. He studied the sign languages of Europe and then helped develop American Sign Language. In 1817, he opened the first American school for the deaf, and in 1864, he established Gallaudet College, in Washington, D.C.

## MAKE A FLAG ALPHABET

**H**ere's an alphabet entirely in flags. For more than two hundred years, the flag alphabet has been a way for sailors to communicate to shore or to another ship. In times of trouble, people can usually see flags before they can hear a shout.

Now electronic communications have mostly replaced the flag alphabet. But sailors still like to know how to talk with flags. When modern equipment fails, the flags are still a good communication backup. You never know when they might come in handy.

The British Navy's flag system calls for 26 flags onboard ship, one for each letter of the alphabet.

The U.S. Navy decided on a different approach. A sailor holds red and yellow flags, one in each hand. The position of the flags say the letter of the alphabet. As the sailor changes the positions, the flags spell out one word after another.

If you want to learn the flag alphabet, you can use any flags just for practice. See how fast you can spell out your message.

### WORD WIZARDRY

The flag alphabet is an example of *semaphores,* a way of communicating by objects such as flags, lights, or the mechanical arms on railroads. Semaphores are often a good code, since not everybody knows what they mean. At the beginning of the Revolutionary War, the American patriot Paul Revere decided on a code of lanterns. One lantern lit in the tower of the Old North Church in Boston meant the British were coming by land. Two lanterns meant by sea. The Americans hoped the British soldiers would not even notice the lights in the tower.

# MAKE A FLAG ALPHABET

### *continued*

### *Here's how to say something important in the flag alphabet:*

· · · · · · · ·
# CREATE ALPHABET ORNAMENTS
· · · · · · · · · · · · · · · · · · ·

**W**ould you like to shape and decorate colorful alphabet ornaments? Perhaps you would like to create the letters for the names of a new school, a new baby, or your whole family. You could use your letters to decorate a holiday centerpiece, a doorknob, or a Christmas tree.

You cook dough to make these letters, but you can't eat them. You won't want to eat them, anyway, when you see how beautiful they are.

### Here's what you need:

*2 cups (0.5 liter) flour*

*2 cups (0.5 liter) water*

*1 cup (0.25 liter) salt*

*2 tablespoons (15 milliliters) cream of tartar*

*Ribbon, string, or wire, if you wish to hang the ornaments*

*Water or tempera paints, with brushes*

*Clear shellac, if you wish*

### Here's what you do:

1. In a medium pan, mix together flour, water, salt, and cream of tartar.

2. Place the pan over medium heat. Stir the mixture constantly, until it is thick. Be patient!

3. Put the pan aside, and let the dough cool until it's safe to handle.

4. Use your hands to shape the dough into letters of the alphabet. If you want to hang the letters (perhaps on a doorknob or a Christmas tree), this is the time to shape the dough around a ribbon, string, or wire.

5. Let the dough letters dry for at least 24 hours.

6. Paint the letters with water or tempera paints. Let dry again.

7. Brush them with clear shellac, if you wish. That helps them last longer.

. . . . . . . .
## CREATE ALPHABET ORNAMENTS
### *continued*

### WORD WIZARDRY

Where would you go to look for a lost letter of the alphabet? Most of our alphabet originated with the ancient Romans, but one mysterious letter came from the Anglo-Saxons of northern Europe.

It's a letter that once meant the "th" sound, but in modern times, it's spelled just as "Y."

Where can you find it in English? Look at signs for places that want to seem old-fashioned. It will be replacing "th" in "the." So if you're seeking the mysterious lost letter of the alphabet, you may find it in "Ye Olde Antiques Shoppe" or "Ye Olde Inn."

. . . . . . . .
## PLAY WITH THE ALPHABET
. . . . . . . . . . . . . . . . . . . .

This is a good way to teach the alphabet to small children. Let them play and shape letters.

### *Here's what you need:*

*2 cups (0.5 liter) flour*
*1 cup (0.25 liter) salt*
*1 cup (0.25 liter) water*
*1 teaspoon (5 milliliters) vegetable oil*
*Food coloring*

### *Here's what you do:*

1. In a large bowl, stir together flour, salt, water, and oil. If the dough is too sticky to handle, add more flour, a tablespoon at a time.

2. Stir in a few drops of food coloring. Then, if you want a deeper color, stir in a few more drops. If you want several colors, divide the dough into small bowls and use a different food coloring for each bowl.

Now go ahead with shaping the dough into letters of the alphabet.

· · · · · · · ·
# EAT THE ALPHABET
· · · · · · · · · · · · · · · · · · ·

These letters of the alphabet are delicious. They're pretzel letters. They're fun to shape. Then you can serve them as refreshments at any special occasion for Word Wizards.

### Here's what you need:

*1¼ cups (0.3 liter) warm water*

*1 tablespoon (1 package or 10 milliliters) yeast*

*1 teaspoon (5 milliliters) sugar*

*3½ to 4 cups (0.85 to 1 liter) flour*

*¼ teaspoon (2 milliliters) salt*

*1 egg yolk*

*2 tablespoons (15 milliliters) water*

*Kosher or other coarse salt*

### Here's what you do:

1. In a large bowl, mix together warm water, yeast, and sugar.

2. Sift flour into another large bowl, and stir in salt.

3. Pour the yeast mixture over the flour. Use a large spoon to mix until the dough is stiff.

4. Turn the dough onto a floured board or pastry cloth. Roll out the dough to about ½ inch thick. Cut into strips about 1 by 3 inches (3 by 8 centimeters).

5. Now roll each dough piece into a thin strip. Then shape each into a letter of the alphabet.

6. Arrange the pretzel letters on a lightly greased baking sheet.

7. Use a fork to beat the egg yolk with 2 tablespoons water. Brush each pretzel with the egg yolk mixture.

8. Sprinkle with kosher or other coarse salt.

9. Cover with a clean towel, and let rise for about ½ hour.

10. Bake in a 400-degree oven about 20 minutes, until pretzels are golden brown.

### WORD WIZARDRY

While you're shaping a pretzel alphabet, perhaps you'll find the answer to this alphabet mystery. Look at these letters, especially while you are shaping them:

A H I M O T U V W X Y

How are these letters alike? See answer on page 205.

. . . . . . . .

# ANSWERS, CHAPTER 10
# SOLVE ALPHABET MYSTERIES

. . . . . . . . . . . . . . . . . . . .

### *Design Your Own Word Pictures:*

Here's how the logograms match up:

| | | | |
|---|---|---|---|
| $ | Dollar sign | % | Percent |
| # | Pound sign | & | And |
| | (meaning a number, | = | Equals |
| | as in #5, or weight in pounds, | ÷ | Divided by |
| | as in 5#, or a symbol on | © | Copyright |
| | a telephone keypad) | | |

### *Play a Game with the Alphabet, and C-D-C Besides:*

Here's how to figure the silly alphabet:

**1. A Silly Seashore Verse**

A sailor went to sea, sea, sea
To see what he could see, see, see.
But all that he could see, see, see
Was the bottom of the great blue sea, sea, sea.

**2. A Conversation at a Restaurant**

Have you any eggs?
Oh yes, we have eggs.
Have you any ham?
Oh yes, we have ham.
OK, I'll have ham and eggs.

**3. A Slogan for Word Wizards**

Excel with ease.

**4. What Happens When You're a Word Wizard**

You are wise.

### *Eat the Alphabet:*

The letters (A, H, I, M, O, T, U, V, W, X, Y) are all mirror-image letters. They are shaped the same, forward and backward.

# 11. Discover Deep Dark Word Secrets

**Easy Q:** What is a noun?

**Easy A:** The name of a person, place, or thing.

**Next Q:** What's in a name?

*T*hat's not so simple. If you look through a standard dictionary, you may find "Jessica" and "Andrew," but not "McNally" or "Zhu." You will find place-names like "New York," but not "Cedar Rapids."

Ordinary dictionaries don't include a complete list of nouns like these, because they can't. There are millions of proper names, each with a set of meanings so complicated that there's no way to create a short, simple definition.

But think about the "Play Name Games" (page 6) and "Get Inside Your Own Name" (page 12), and then look at "Become the Private Eye of Words" on page 214. You'll find ways to go beyond the dictionary and see into the deeper, stranger meanings of names. Actually, you can do the same with almost any word in English, and if you poke down far enough, you'll start to find meanings few people ever see.

You'll see into the sources for your town's name, for words that English has borrowed from other languages, and for words that most people will never understand. You'll see into words that are really lies, and others that are complete nonsense.

You'll be a detective with words, digging down into them.

. . . . . . . .

# SEE WHAT'S BEHIND YOUR TOWN'S NAME

. . . . . . . . . . . . . . . . . . . .

| Reason | Maybe | Likely | Definitely |
|---|---|---|---|
| Pure accident | | | |
| First settlers' family name | | | |
| Copied from Europe | | | |
| Native American word | | | |
| Natural surroundings | | | |
| Religion | | | |
| Local work done | | | |
| Local animal or tree | | | |

**W**hoever they were, the founders of your town probably named it for at least one of the eight reasons above, including "pure accident." Most towns don't have single, clear ideas behind their names, and if you ask, most people living around you will give you different explanations for the town's name.

Maybe there's not much mystery if you live in Shoemakersville, Pennsylvania, or Kit Carson, Colorado. But what about Medicine Hat, Alberta; or Peru, Indiana; or Clarinda, Iowa? It's not so easy to put check marks in the boxes for towns like those.

Try it for your town. Mark all the boxes that seem to make sense to you, then check out this way of digging deeper.

........
# SEE WHAT'S BEHIND YOUR TOWN'S NAME
## *continued*

### Here's what you need:

*A few talks with older relatives
  or neighbors*
*One trip to the local library*

### Here's what you do:

1. Think about the check marks you made, especially if you're not 100 percent sure that there's one clear reason for the town's name. Then think about who might know more, particularly if you have older relatives who live in town.

2. The next time you see the older people, show them your check marks and ask:

   - Have you ever heard another explanation that you believe could be true?

   - Far back in history, did the town ever have a different name? If so, what changed it?

   - If the name came from Europe, where is the original town? Why did the first settlers here choose to copy that town's name instead of another's?

   - Do you think most adults here could really explain the town's name?

3. When you have all the information you can get, go talk to a librarian. Most libraries have plenty of maps, histories, and letters from the early days of local towns. You'll have fun checking into the stories you've heard, and you'll probably find that you need to erase some of your first check marks and put in a few new ones.

Then let your relatives know what you've found. They'll like learning how right they were.

### WORD WIZARDRY

Names of five real places in North America:

Bird-in-Hand, Pennsylvania
Lake Oblivion, New Brunswick
Red Jacket, West Virginia
Dinkytown, Minnesota
Come by Chance, Newfoundland

# SNIFF OUT A SNAFU

SNAFU = *S*ituation *N*ormal, *A*ll *F*ouled *U*p

**D**uring the First and Second World Wars, U.S. soldiers invented *snafu,* a new word for the problems of trying to get ready to go into action. To them, a snafu could mean anything from bad weather to missing ammunition to spoiled food.

Words like *snafu* are called acronyms. They work as quick, useful ways to shorten phrases, and they often become part of written and spoken English. But today many people feel that English is getting overloaded with acronyms. Maybe we use them too often as substitutes for real words.

Judge for yourself, because there's a good way to investigate acronyms. You can see how many you already know, and decide whether they're really helpful. You can also work with your friends to try inventing better ones.

## Here's what you need:

*Pencil and paper*
*A talk with two or three friends*

## Here's what you do:

**1.** See if you can match up the acronyms and meanings on this list. One is done for you.

| Acronyms | Meanings | Acronyms | Meanings |
|---|---|---|---|
| 1. GI (H) | A. Radio detection and ranging | 6. DOS ( ) | F. American League |
| 2. SUV ( ) | B. Disk operating system | 7. Radar ( ) | G. Digital videodisc |
| 3. AOK ( ) | C. Keyboard layout | 8. PC ( ) | H. Government issue |
| 4. AL ( ) | D. Sport utility vehicle | 9. Qwerty ( ) | I. Personal computer |
| 5. Y2K ( ) | E. Perfectly good | 10. DVD ( ) | J. The year 2000 |

· · · · · · · ·

# SNIFF OUT A SNAFU
## *continued*

Maybe you did this very quickly and got all the answers on page 227. But no matter how many you got, look back at the list.

2. Notice how acronyms are usually made. Like *snafu,* they combine the first letters of the real words that you could use for the meaning. Those letters usually come in order and can be spoken.

   But notice also that some, like *qwerty,* don't obey those rules at all.

3. Now think about what you might have to do to invent an acronym. Is there something you can put together that would become popular? Is there a situation you and your friends see all the time that could be abbreviated? Would it have to follow the rules for acronyms? For a start, talk over ideas like these. See what comes to you.

| | |
|---|---|
| being late all the time | losing important papers |
| always being first | daydreaming |
| liking all kinds of animals | being extremely neat |
| wearing nice clothes | liking sports |

If you got eight or more of the acronyms on the first list and if you're now finding it easy to think up new ones, maybe there's something to that theory about English getting overloaded.

Y, U could even put up a BBS to answer FAQs about it ASAP.

### WORD WIZARDRY

In Latin, the word *acer* means "sharp." So in English, we now have *acronyms,* which are short, "sharp" ways to refer to ideas too awkward to spell out in detail. *Scuba* works much better than "**s**elf-**c**ontained **u**nderwater **b**reathing **a**pparatus," doesn't it?

. . . . . . . .
# PACK UP YOUR PORTMANTEAU
. . . . . . . . . . . . . . . . . . . .

**O**n pages 48 to 72, you can see dozens of ways to string words together artistically, to create different kinds of poems, lyrics, and stories. But here's a way to do something inventive with just *one* word.

What you do is think up something called a portmanteau word. That's pronounced port-MAN-toe, and it's an old-fashioned way of saying "suitcase." The idea behind it is to jam two meanings into one word, so that it works like a suitcase holding them.

*Smog* is a portmanteau word, because it combines the terms *smoke* and *fog*. *Brunch* would be another one, because *breakfast* and *lunch* are put together to create a new word that anybody can understand.

. . . . . . . .

# PACK UP YOUR PORTMANTEAU

## *continued*

Think about trying it yourself. What can you do to fill in the list?

| Portmanteau Word | First Meaning | Second Meaning |
| --- | --- | --- |
| fanzine | magazine | for fans |
| Chunnel | tunnel | under the English Channel |
| ? | comedy | situation |
| ? | video camera | video recorder |
| ? | man who works too hard | ? |
| ? | big view of the sea | ? |

And keep going. If you have enough fun with this, maybe you will invent four or five new Wizwords that people will actually start using.

### WORD WIZARDRY

Portmanteau words often get invented to describe a new trend. In the 1920s, many Americans were starting to drive **mot**or cars to faraway places, and they wanted small ho**tels** along the roads. So *motels* started getting built.

· · · · · · ·
# BECOME THE PRIVATE EYE OF WORDS
· · · · · · · · · · · · · · · · ·

ENTYMOLOGIST

ETYMOLOGIST

**Q:** What's the difference?
**A:** Ask her.

**E**tymologists don't just know how to define words. They go much further, checking into where, when, and why words were invented. And with English, that can get to be a strange job, because so much of the language is mysterious.

But big parts of English are also perfectly clear. Many of our words are based directly on the Greek, Latin, and German spoken centuries ago, and some haven't changed much at all. Look at these three.

| English Word | Ancient Source | What It Meant |
|---|---|---|
| telephone | Greek | tele = over a distance<br>phone = hear, speak, or understand |
| student | Latin | studiere = to study<br>ent = someone who does that |
| church | Old German | kirk = church |

· · · · · · · ·
# BECOME THE PRIVATE EYE OF WORDS
## *continued*

For etymologists, though, the fun starts when word sources aren't so clear. What etymologists try to do is figure out how odd words have managed to get into English by being "borrowed." That can mean looking into the cases of words that have been stolen, changed, improved, or even totally misunderstood as they've moved into English.

Investigating words yourself can be fun. There's no magnifying glass, but you do work like a private eye, and you handle some strange cases.

### Here's what you need:

*A complete, full-size English dictionary*
*A tablet and pencil*

### Here's what you do:

1. Sit down with the biggest dictionary you can find. If you don't have a big dictionary at home, go to your school or public library's reference desk and ask for one.
2. Write the word *nice* at the top of one page in your tablet. Then write *trivial* on a second page and *macaroni* on a third.
3. Look up *nice.* You'll find something like seven or eight meanings for it, plus some clues that it once meant something *not* "nice" in Latin and Old French. Start noting down the old meanings, spellings, and pronunciations in columns, like this. And see how much information the dictionary gives you to fill in the "?" boxes.

**Nice**

| Language | Word | Meaning | Pronounced |
|---|---|---|---|
| Latin | nescire | not knowing, or ignorant | nay-SKEE-ray, or nay-SHEE-ray |
| Old French | niche | stupid | neesh |
| ? | ? | ? | ? |
| ? | ? | ? | ? |
| Modern English | nice | good, or pleasant | nīs |

········
# BECOME THE PRIVATE EYE OF WORDS
## *continued*

If your dictionary is complete enough, you'll find that the word *nice* was picked up by Middle English in about the year 1300, to mean not just "stupid," but "too open." But then, in the years between 1400 and 1700, it also came to mean "shy," "dainty," and "precise" as English changed. And today we have "good." By 2100, who knows?

**4.** Do the same work with *trivial* and *macaroni.* If you check into *macaroni* enough, you'll learn why Yankee Doodle had to give his feather a name.

Keep on with your private-eye work if you like the idea of discovering the real sources of modern English. After you see enough patterns like the ones behind *nice,* you'll develop a feeling for the old meanings.

### WORD WIZARDRY

Deep in the past, few people went to schools and learned how to write. So they thought that writing was a mysterious, magical, beautiful thing to do. And they began to invent words for it, including *glamorous.*

| Years | Languages | Words |
|-----------|------------|---------------------------|
| 100–700 | Latin | grammatica |
| 700–1300 | Old French | gramaire |
| 1500–1800 | Scottish | glamourie |
| 1800–now | English | grammar (and glamour) |

........

# DECIPHER THE DICTIONARY

. . . . . . . . . . . . . . . . . . . .

Look up the word *dog* in the printed or CD dictionary that you use most often. You'll find something like this:

> **dog** \do̊g\ n **1a** a variable flesh-eating domesticated mammal probably descended from the common wolf **b** an animal of the family to which the domesticated dog belongs **c** a male dog **2** a worthless fellow **3** any of various devices for holding, gripping, or fastening that consist of a spike, rod, or bar . . . [Old English *dogca*].

Phew! Maybe that's too much.

But if you were in charge of the dictionary, what would you do? The purpose of a dictionary is to show what a word means, and most words don't cooperate. They have at least two or three meanings, and many times no logic links any one of those to the others.

So dictionary editors try to use a system, to put the most usual, general meaning first. When most people say "dog," they mean the animal, so that shows up as the **1a**, **b**, and **c** you see in the sample above. But we also say things like "He's a lazy dog," and so that becomes the **2** you see. The **3** shows you a special meaning, one that carpenters and metalworkers use to describe a rod or a plug that holds their work in place.

Other dictionaries list meanings by their historical order, with oldest meanings first, even if those meanings are not the most ordinary usages now.

When you use your dictionary, always look at all the meanings. That way, you'll be sure to know how a word is most often used, plus what it *can* mean when used in a different way.

And try this, because you'll see something else about dictionaries.

········
# DECIPHER THE DICTIONARY
### *continued*

## What Does the Word *School* Mean?

| Number? | Meaning | Number? | Meaning |
|---------|---------|---------|---------|
| | place where education happens | | fish swimming together |
| | a style of art or thought | | a tradition |
| | (as a verb) to train | | (as an adjective) belonging to or appropriate to young people |

After you decide which meaning is **1**, and which are **2–6**, think about the words shown on the right. Is there a way you can make them more exact, so that nobody seeing your total definition would be confused?

After all, a student could be *schooled* as an actor to take part in a *school* play being held at *school,* with the same word being used as a verb, an adjective, and a noun. So to make things clear, you need to work carefully on the "Meaning" column.

That has always been the hardest part of the job, even for professional dictionary editors. Take Noah Webster, who was the most important dictionary editor for the English you speak. In 1783, he published *The Blue-Backed Speller,* the first book showing Americans how to spell words in a standard way. At the time, people here had no rules for spelling, and a word like *public* was also written as *publick* and *publique.*

It took Webster another 45 years to finish the first complete dictionary of American English.

### WORD WIZARDRY

Pay attention to the terms like [Old English *dogca*] in your dictionary. A good private eye of words has to recognize ancient English, too.

# LOAD UP YOUR WIZARD'S MEMORY BANK

**O**ne reason for the strength of modern English is that it has absorbed so much. We've filled it up with thousands of foreign words, such as *tortilla, wok, algebra, beau,* and *kaput.* We've also been good at reinventing words, to cover everything from a computer *mouse* to a TV *remote* to a football *coach.*

English grows and changes every day, mostly for the better. But it has problems, too, because its rules for spelling and writing aren't always clear or systematic. Learning the basic rules is easy enough, but even a simple word like *friend* can show how unpredictable English is. You don't hear the *i* in the word, and no particular rule helps you to avoid wrong spellings like *frend* or *freind.* You just have to memorize *friend,* or remember the rough rule that says, "*i* before *e,* except after *c.*" But even that's a problem, because it doesn't work for *seize* or *being.*

Recognizing correct English takes concentration, even if it's just for the half-second needed to memorize a word. Maybe that's why there's so much bad English around, and why so many people don't bother to get words right. You've probably seen plenty like these.

········

# LOAD UP YOUR WIZARD'S MEMORY BANK
## *continued*

| | |
|---|---|
| Puppys' 4 Sale | Take You're Seat |
| luvya alot | he or she and there friends |
| Seperate Your Recyclabels | your alright |
| Orange's 2.49$ doz. | ‛!' *!* ☺ |

At least the little faces are cute. All the others are simple misspellings or clumsy substitutes for perfectly good English. But many people don't even try to do better, and some have probably gotten so used to incorrect English that they don't notice.

Word Wizards do notice, though. Correct English is in their heads, and getting it in there is easy enough to do.

### Here's what you need:

*Four blank pages in the back of a notebook*

*A regular pencil and a colored pencil*

*A ruler*

### Here's what you do:

1. Use the ruler and the regular pencil to divide each page into three vertical columns. Make the left and center columns each 2 inches (5 centimeters) wide, and leave the rest of the space for the right column.

   With the regular pencil, write in "Wrong," "Right," and "Why" as headlines for the three columns, working from left to right.

2. Then look at the incorrect samples above and pick out your two favorites. Copy each of them into the "Wrong" column in clear letters, just as they appear.

3. Think about each of them for a minute to determine exactly why they're wrong. If you picked "Take You're Seat," for example, you probably realized that "You're" is the problem and that "Your" would be the correct version. But why?

   Look at it this way. The apostrophe mark (') does only two things in correct written English:

   • It stands for missing letters, letting us write words like *don't* instead of *do not*.

# LOAD UP YOUR WIZARD'S MEMORY BANK
## *continued*

- Or it shows possession, so we can use *Juan's bike* instead of *the bike of Juan*.

So there's no way for "Take You're Seat" to be correct. It can't mean "Take You Are Seat," because that makes no sense, and it can't mean "Take the Seat of You," because the *e* in "You're" makes the spelling wrong.

4. Now expand your thinking. Have you seen other words that seem repeatedly misused? Think about what you see in ads, in notes from your friends, on signs, and on Web sites, plus what you hear in conversations or on radio.

Write three or four of the most obviously incorrect ones into the "Wrong" column, and use the colored pencil to mark exactly where the errors occur.

5. Then use your regular pencil to fill in corrected versions under "Right," and pay attention to the odd feeling that will probably develop. You'll sense that somehow, you actually do know what's right, even though you may not know exactly why.

But think about it. What can you put in the "Why" column for each error you chose?

- Are there simple, "unofficial" rules that occur to you right away?

- Can you write them under "Why" in your own words?

- Would your own rules work for most or all mistakes like the ones you chose?

If you spend some time working on "Why," you'll get paid back in at least three important ways. First, you'll realize how much of a Word Wizard you already are, because growing up with a language means that you develop a general and powerful *feeling* for it. Second, you'll see how unconsciously your sense of language grows, like your feeling for throwing or dancing. Third, you'll see that once you get it right, good English does stay with you. Bad disappears.

### WORD WIZARDRY

*Wuts* on *you're* list? *Alot* of words *youll* never get *mixedup becuase theyre fix'ed* now? Or a good way to see into what's right and what isn't?

········

# Do English a Favor

· · · · · · · · · · · · · · · · · · · · · ·

**S**ay you're standing outside school, waiting for a ride home.

Would you also be anticipating the arrival of the personal transportation necessary to effect your transfer from a learning environment to the family residence?

Let's hope not, because no reasonable person thinks that way. But unfortunately, more and more people do seem to believe that plain English isn't good enough for what they need to say. So instead of *jail,* they might use *correctional institution, rehabilitative facility,* or even *behavior modification center.* They assume that big, difficult words somehow make their ideas more impressive.

But usually what happens is the reverse. Overcomplicated English just seems awkward, and using odd words instead of plain ones can subtract more meaning than it adds. To see how that works and to have some fun with it, consider what might happen if you started a campaign called Plain English Power.

One step could be writing letters and E-mails like the ones on pages 111 and 177. Another could be an agreement with your friends to stage a more direct attack on the problem.

SANITATION ENGINEER
(GARBAGE MAN)

. . . . . . . .
# DO ENGLISH A FAVOR
## *continued*

### *Here's what you need:*

*At least three friends who are good at making jokes on the spot*
*An agreement with them to make fun of bad English whenever it shows up*

### *Here's what you do:*

1. Ask your friends to think over three questions.
   - Do we know particular people who often try to make themselves seem important by using big words?
   - What are their favorite sayings?
   - What if we translated those sayings into totally plain English?
2. Have the group look over this list. It may give you a few ideas about who the people could be.

| Bad English Version | Actual Meaning |
|---|---|
| complete satisfaction with your dining experience | good meal |
| assessing the multiple alternatives involved at this time | thinking about |
| important members of the school's extended family | parents |
| giving 110 percent on every play, every way, every day | trying hard |
| full-service provider of financial solutions | bank |
| distinctive excellence, for the discerning purchaser | expensive |

· · · · · · · ·
# DO ENGLISH A FAVOR
### *continued*

**3.** If you found it easy to imagine a restaurant manager saying the first line, and a coach who talks like the fourth, you shouldn't have too much trouble picking out the real people who need your help.

Decide on two or three in your neighborhood or at school, each one known for a favorite saying that's awkward and overcomplicated.

**4.** Then work with your friends to translate the sayings into just one or two plain words.

Once you have the short versions, make an agreement that each of you will seek out chances to use them, right on the spot.

Here's an example. If a person you've chosen always says something like "We all share in a continuing responsibility to maintain the building's safety and appearance," that's the right moment for you to step in and apply some Plain English Power. You say— *"Don't litter!"*

If you do that often enough, you'll slowly start to have an effect. Some people will laugh right away and agree that you've caught them. Others will need longer, but there's plenty of value in keeping at Plain English Power.

Someday, you and your friends might even create a world where school days could start with a class and end with a game. You wouldn't have to participate in a discovery module occurring prior to a scheduled inter-scholastic competition.

### WORD WIZARDRY

Awkward ways to say "thanks":
  Please accept my appreciation.
  I owe you a debt of gratitude.
  Your cooperation has been
    invaluable.
  Your assistance is much
    appreciated.

# DRAW PUN PICTURES

WHOA!
BIGFELLA CRUM!

**I**f you like cartooning, here's a way to base it on something completely unpredictable: words.

Look at the girl in the cartoon, the one whose head is covered with rabbits. For some reason she's using a calculator. What's she doing?

She's trying to figure out how many *hares* are on her head, and she's paying no attention to the pigeon who's talking *Pidgin*.

Both jokes work because they're visual puns. They depend on words called homonyms, which sound exactly the same but have different meanings and spellings.

Turning homonyms into cartoons takes them one step further. Because the words themselves are just suggested by the cartoon, the person seeing it can't get the joke without guessing that it's based on sound-alike words.

Here's a short list of homonyms to consider. Think up a few of your own, add them into the blanks, and then take another look at the full list. What do you see for cartoon possibilities? Are two or three good enough to give people a laugh?

| | | |
|---|---|---|
| paste . . . paced | chilly . . . chili . . . Chile | beat . . . beet |
| bowled . . . bold | I'll . . . aisle . . . isle | rose . . . rows |
| _____ . . . _____ | _____ . . . _____ | _____ . . . _____ |
| _____ . . . _____ | _____ . . . _____ | _____ . . . _____ |

### WORD WIZARDRY

Check around for a copy of Lewis Carroll's *Through the Looking-Glass.* You'll get new ideas about how to link up strange art with even stranger words.

# TWIST AND RETWIST TONGUE TWISTERS

*She sells seashells down by the seashore.*
*He brings brick-baked black bread.*
*Zithers slither slowly south, shyly hither, slyly thither, never nether.*

**A**t first, talking your way through tongue twisters seems hard. The syllables bang up against each other, and usually you need three or four tries to get them straight.

But if you look closely enough at written versions, you'll see right away how tongue twisters work. You'll also see how to get good at them and how to think up new ones to try on your friends. Look at this:

Z**ith**ers sl**ith**er slowly **south**, shyly **hith**er, slyly **thith**er, n**ever neth**er.

The sounds in bold type are all slight variations on the sound of "ith," put so close together that they're hard to say smoothly. And the tangle of "sl," "sh," and "n" sounds doesn't help. Your mouth has to work hard.

But there is a way to get them untangled. All you have to do is practice it a few times, and you'll see how to handle almost any tongue twister. Say this out loud, but *slowly:*

*She sells . . . seashells . . . down by . . . the seashore.*

Suddenly, it's easy. Try it twice more, slightly faster each time, and you'll see that getting good isn't so hard. Just a little practice does it, and you can go on to try harder ones the same way.

To have fun with your friends, give them a few like these. All you need to do is fit some new problems into an old tongue twister, or invent something nobody's heard before.

*She **should** sell **sillier** seashells **on silver sheets** down by the seashore.*
*She says sick sisters' assistants sit as still as sick assistant sissies.*

After some practice, maybe they'll get as good as you.

. . . . . . . .

# TWIST AND RETWIST TONGUE TWISTERS
## *continued*

### WORD WIZARDRY

Here are eight good sounds to work into tongue twisters. They work because they make your throat, mouth, and tongue move in many different ways. Test them to see how those movements feel. Tongue twisters are more fun if you say them as fast as possible.

| | |
|---|---|
| br | bl |
| th | z |
| sl | sm |
| bo | qu |

. . . . . . . .

# ANSWERS, CHAPTER 11
# DISCOVER DEEP DARK WORD SECRETS

. . . . . . . . . . . . . . . . . . . .

### *Sniff Out a Snafu:*

How did you do with the acronyms on page 210? Here are the answers.

| Acronym | Answer |
|---------|--------|
| GI | H |
| SUV | D |
| AOK | E |
| AL | F |
| Y2K | J |
| DOS | B |
| Radar | A |
| PC | I |
| Qwerty | C |
| DVD | G |

# GLOSSARY

| | |
|---|---|
| **Abcedarium** | A sentence using all 26 letters of the alphabet, often used to learn keyboarding or calligraphy. A *pangram*. |
| **Acronym** | A word formed from the first letters of several words or from the most important letters of several words. An example is *radar*. The letters stand for "<u>ra</u>dio <u>d</u>etection <u>an</u>d <u>r</u>anging." |
| **Alliteration** | Repetition of the sounds of words, usually consonants. Alliteration is often used in titles, poems, and songs. |
| **Alphabet** | A system of writing in which letters represent the sounds of words, vowels, and consonants. An alphabet has a usual order for the letters, such as our alphabet, with its 26 letters arranged A through Z. |
| **American Sign Language** | A system of hand signs that communicate words, sounds, and letters of the alphabet, used by hearing-impaired people in the United States and Canada. Sometimes called *Ameslan*. |
| **Anagram** | A word or message created from another by rearranging the letters. A game of making words by changing, adding, or scrambling letters. |
| **Antonym** | A word that has the opposite meaning of another word. *Cold* is the antonym of *hot*. |
| **Ascender line** | A term in calligraphy for the line above the baseline to which tall letters, such as *d* and *t*, reach. |
| **Baseline** | A term in calligraphy for the line upon which all the letters sit. |
| **Bites** | Short, colorful statements in the media that summarize a story or idea and make it memorable. Also called *sound bites*. |
| **Caesar, Julius** | (100?–44 B.C.). Roman statesman and general. |
| **Calligraphy** | The art of beautiful handwriting. |
| **Character** | An imaginary person in a story, poem, play, movie, or television show. A fictional person. |
| **Cipher** | A way of writing secret messages. A cipher may rearrange or scramble the letters of a message. Or a cipher may substitute other letters, numbers, or symbols for the letters of the message. |
| **Code** | A set of signals, words, or symbols used to send messages. A secret message in which the words or sentences are substitutes for other words and sentences, with secret meanings. |
| **Communication** | The exchange of information and thoughts. A system for transmitting information and ideas, such as telephone or television. The science and art of the interchange of thoughts, ideas, and information. |
| **Creole** | A combination of two or more languages that has developed until it is nearly a separate language on its own. |
| **Descender line** | A term in calligraphy for the line below the baseline to which long letters, such as *p* and *g*, reach. |
| **Eponym** | A word based on the name of a person or place. An example is *sandwich,* based on the title of John Montague, the Earl of Sandwich, |

|  |  |
|---|---|
|  | who in 1762 first called for a quick meal of meat between pieces of bread. Also called an *eponymous word*. |
| **Etymology** | The study of the origin, history, and development of words. |
| **Font** | A complete alphabet or set of type, all in one style. |
| **Format** | The shape, size, arrangement, and general makeup of a publication, such as a book, magazine, or stationery. |
| **Gallaudet, Thomas** | (1787–1851). United States educator and writer who helped to develop American Sign Language and who established the first American schools and college for the deaf. |
| **Glyph** | A sign, symbol, or picture that represents a word, phrase, or message. An icon or symbol that indicates choices on a computer program. |
| **Graffiti** | Pictures or writings on a building or wall, sometimes done secretly or without permission. *Graffiti* is the plural of *graffito*. |
| **Graphology** | The science of analyzing handwriting, in order to learn something about the person who did the writing. Graphology may show whether writing, such as a signature, is genuine or fake. |
| **Gutenberg, Johannes** | (1400–1468). German printer who invented a process of printing from movable type that made inexpensive, wide-scale printing possible. |
| **Haiku** | Traditionally Japanese poems that describe an image in nature or a season. Haiku are written in three lines, with five syllables in the first line, seven syllables in the second line, and five syllables in the third line. |
| **Hieroglyphic** | A picture or symbol that stands for a sound, syllable, word, or idea. Associated with ancient Egypt. |
| **Homonym** | A word that is pronounced the same as another word, but with a different meaning and, often, a different spelling. An example is *hear* and *here*. |
| **Iambic pentameter** | In poetry, a line of five poetic feet, each with a first unaccented or weak syllable followed by one accented or strong syllable. Known as a favorite rhythm for poems in the English language. An example is "To strive, / to seek, / to find, / and not / to yield." |
| **Icon** | A symbol or picture that indicates choices on a computer program. |
| **Isogram** | A word in which no letter of the alphabet is used more than once. An example is the word *isogram* itself. |
| **Language** | Words, with distinct pronunciations and combinations, as used and understood by a large group of people. A systematic means of communication through speech, writing, or signs. |
| **Limerick** | A type of funny verse five lines long. The first, second, and fifth lines all rhyme. The third and fourth verses follow another rhyme. Named after a city in Ireland. |
| **Logo** | A symbol or picture that represents a brand, business, team, or organization. |
| **Logogram** | A symbol, picture, or letter that represents a whole word. An example is $ for dollar. |
| **Lowercase** | Belonging to the alphabet series *a*, *b*, *c* rather than *A*, *B*, *C*. Small letters of the alphabet as distinguished from capital or uppercase letters. Printers once kept these letters in the lower of two type cases. |

**Media**    The means of communication to many people at once, including television, radio, movies, books, newspapers, and magazines.

**Metaphor**    A figure of speech in which one thing is compared directly to another. An example is "All the world's a stage."

**Morse code**    A system of communication consisting of short and long signals or dots and dashes. Morse code can be transmitted by sight or sound. It was originally based on communication by telegraph.

**Morse, Samuel F. B.**    (1791–1872). The inventor of the telegraph and Morse code.

**Nulls**    Meaningless letters, numbers, or symbols inserted into a cipher in order to make the cipher more complicated and difficult.

**Onomatopoeic**    Describing a word that sounds like what it means. An example is *dingdong,* which suggests the sound of a doorbell ringing. Or describing a word that imitates a natural sound, such as *buzz.*

**Palindrome**    A word, phrase, or sentence that reads the same forward or backward, without changing the spelling. An example is Adam's introduction to Eve: "Madam, I'm Adam."

**Pangram**    A sentence that uses each of the 26 letters of the alphabet. Often used as a word game or as a way to learn keyboarding. An *abcedarium.*

**Pen width**    A term in calligraphy for the thickest line the pen can make. A pen width is often used to measure the height and width of letters or the distance between letters and words.

**Pictograph**    A picture or symbol that represents a word or idea. A system of picture writing.

**Pidgin**    A simple combination of two or more languages, often used so that people can do business together, even though they speak different languages.

**Plot**    The plan of action or main story of a literary work, such as a novel, short story, movie, play, or poem.

**Poetry**    Writing that creates an emotional response through meaning, sound, and rhythm.

**Point of type**    A measure of type used in printing, equal to about $1/72$ inch, or less than 0.5 millimeter.

**Portmanteau word**    A word that combines two or more words. *Portmanteau* originally meant a type of suitcase. An example is *sitcom,* a combination of *situation* and *comedy.*

**Pun**    A joking way of using a word so as to suggest two different meanings, or of using words that sound nearly the same but have different meanings. A play on words. An example is referring to the "hares on your head" as if they were rabbits.

**Rebus**    A puzzle or riddle made up of pictures that suggest words. An example is the picture of a heart used to indicate love.

**Rhyme**    Ends of words that sound alike, such as *star* and *far.* Verse or poetry written so that the sounds at the end of each line sound alike.

**Semaphore**    A system for sending a message with objects, such as flags, lights, or the mechanical arms at railroad crossings. A semaphore can be a code, such as Paul Revere's lanterns in the church tower to signal whether the British were coming by land or by sea.

**Senryu**  Traditionally Japanese poems, written in the same style as haiku, but taking any subject, even humorous subjects. Named for the poet who developed them.

**Sequoyah**  (1770?–1843) Cherokee Indian scholar who invented a writing system for the Cherokee nation and who established the first newspapers and books in the Cherokee language.

**Setting**  The place, surroundings, time, and background for a literary work, such as a novel, short story, movie, play, or poem.

**Signet**  A seal or mark used instead of a handwritten signature.

**Simile**  A figure of speech that compares one thing to another by using the words *like* or *as*. An example is "She is as bright as an April morning."

**SOS**  The way to call for help in Morse code. The letters do not stand for words, but translate to three short, three long, three short.

**Substitution cipher**  A way of sending secret messages in which the letters of the message are replaced by other letters, numbers, or symbols.

**Syllabary**  A system of writing, in which symbols stand for syllables rather than for separate sounds.

**Symmetry**  A balance or pattern in which one part closely resembles another part. The wings of a butterfly show symmetry. A poem or a song can show symmetry by repetition and pattern.

**Synonym**  A word that has the same or almost the same meaning as another word. *Big* is a synonym for *large*.

**Tongue twister**  A phrase or sentence that is difficult to pronounce because of a number of nearly similar sounds. An example is "She sells seashells down by the seashore."

**Transposition cipher**  A way of sending secret messages in which the letters of the message are scrambled.

**Uppercase**  Belonging to the alphabet series *A, B, C* rather than *a, b, c*. The capital letters of the alphabet. Printers once kept these letters in the upper of two type cases.

**Webster, Noah**  (1758–1843). The dictionary maker, author, and editor who compiled the first American dictionary and who first standardized American spelling, pronunciation, and usage.

**X-Line**  A term in calligraphy for the height above the baseline to which letters such as *x* reach. These are letters that do not go up or down.

# RESOURCES FOR WORD WIZARDS

This book is about doing things for yourself. But there can come a time when you ought to have help. You may be looking for help on a computer, at school, at a library, or around home. Wherever you look, you need resources you can count on. Here's how to find what you need.

Don't use the same dictionary all the time. Instead, find the right dictionary. Here's how to tell if you have the right dictionary for your purpose:

1. Once in a while, you may want to look at a huge dictionary. Your local or school library may have a dictionary so big and heavy that you can hardly lift it. You can find just about anything in it, especially if you like old-fashioned words and unusual words. If you want to see if a dictionary includes uncommon or out-of-date words, look to see if it includes words like *grig, Cinerama,* or *zizith.* (A grig is a small lively person or sometimes a small lively creature such as a grasshopper or a cricket. The Cinerama was a type of wide-angle movie screen, rarely in use anymore. Zizith [pronounced tsē-sēt] refers to the distinctive fringes or tassels at the ends of prayer shawls worn by many Jews.)

2. If you want to check that a dictionary is up-to-date, look up recently invented words like *database* or *googol* or a word with modern meanings, such as *computer.* (The word *computer* used to refer to a person who did computing, not a machine.) Or look up modern spellings of place names. An up-to-date dictionary ought to refer to the Chinese city *Beijing,* not *Peking,* which is the old spelling.

3. If you're a Word Wizard, you may want to consult a dictionary that tells you the history of any word you like and the way the meaning of a word changes over time. If you're checking to see if a dictionary is good at this sort of information, look up the history of the word *nice* or *OK.* (OK—often spelled out as okay—is used around the world in virtually every language, but no one is quite sure what the initials mean.)

4. Or you may want to look at a small specialty dictionary, the sort of dictionary that treats one subject. You can find just the right dictionary for nearly any subject that interests you: slang, rhymes, sports, science,

math, medical terms, sign language, or foreign language translation. Check for quality by looking up a term you already know and seeing if the definition is clear and complete—and perhaps tells you something new. For example, check a dictionary of slang to see if it includes slang you already know, such as the new meanings of the word *awesome* or *hanging.* (Remember that young people are usually the ones who originate new slang and who change word meanings. You may know more about changes in language than your parents and teachers—and your own knowledge may sometimes be more up-to-date than a lot of dictionaries.)

5. You may want to know about Word Wizard controversies. Some dictionaries tell you about disagreements in how a word is spelled or pronounced—or arguments about exactly what a word means and what could be the future of a word. Some dictionaries tell you about changes in word usage. Some include charts that help you figure out alphabets, punctuation, measuring and numbering systems, abbreviations, and foreign phrases. To check the quality of a dictionary, see if it gives you a clear distinction between the words *farther* and *further,* or between *imply* and *infer.*

6. If you have a computer, you may want to own a dictionary disk. Make sure the disk is comprehensive and up-to-date, just as you should when you look at any other dictionary. Information presented in a new and interesting way is not necessarily new and correct information.

Besides finding words in dictionaries of all sorts, a Word Wizard ought to look at a thesaurus once in a while, either in a book or on a computer. A thesaurus is a book of synonyms. You think of a word close to the word you want, and the thesaurus helps you find just the right word. To check the quality of a thesaurus, look up words similar to the words *lofty, fair, tease,* or *conventional.*

A Word Wizard may also want to go beyond dictionaries and other reference books. You can go directly to an original resource. You may want to do research in town records (on a subject like place names, for example) or talk to people who know about your subject from personal experience.

Most of all, a Word Wizard needs to take in words, words everywhere. The more good books you read, the more you will absorb about language, poetry, and words—and any other subject. If you're a Word Wizard, you always have plenty of interesting resources.

# INDEX